SECOND EDITION

Notes
from
My Bible

J. Gordon Henry, Ed.D.

Other books by J. Gordon Henry
A Christian's Necessary Food
Adoration: Prayer as Worship
The Enabler
Intercession: Prayer as Work
Prayer Seminar Workbook
Spiritual Warfare
The Model Prayer
Upper Room Discourse

Dedication

To the memory of our parents:
Ira Mae Covington Henry (1899-1970)
Lee Henry, Sr. (1900-1984)

Willie Clark King Troutman (1911-1992)
Rollie A. Troutman (1904-1994)

whose lives inspire us to
serve the Lord Jesus Christ wholeheartedly and
whose memories make us
homesick for Heaven,
our eternal Home.

A Word to the Reader

Since November 1983, as a feature of the *Reflector*, I have shared *Notes from My Bible*—the harvest of forty-seven years of walking with God gathering flowers from many gardens. Clearly understand that most of these are not original. During the course of my study, I have tried to gather "nuggets" and make note of them. I have found this to be a helpful habit which preserves for use many apt sayings and seed thoughts that would have otherwise been forgotten.

Someone has said that there are two kinds of reading—*"reading on a sofa and reading with a pencil in hand."* I long ago learned to read with a pen or pencil in my hand. Scarcely a day has passed since 1977 that I have not entered some note or notes into my Bible. I never read a book without taking notes for preservation one way or another.

You will grow more deeply interested in your Bible day by day if you will make notes in the margins and on blank leaves of your Bible. Staying in the Word daily is so very important that my advice to believers is that if there are days when you have to choose how to use your time—either praying or reading the Bible—to read the Bible. It is far more important for you to hear what God has to say to you than for God to hear what you have to say to Him. Think about that for a moment. Do you really believe that God speaks out of His Word? It is doubtful that any person will ever become a prayer warrior or be Spirit-filled (**Ephesians 5:18**) who does not get into the Word of God on a daily basis. Taking notes will help and you will be surprised at how your prayer life will be strengthened when you develop a working knowledge of the Word of God!

To encourage Bible reading and note-taking, I pass around samples of study Bibles which I have marked to illustrate the helpfulness of taking notes. Each time I pick up the Bible to read, I have a pen or pencil and many times a six-inch very thin ruler. As the Holy Spirit impresses thoughts in my mind, I underline or circle—key words, key phrases, key verses, or key passages. Often I make a note in the margin of thoughts which come as I read. Since the tendency would be to depend on notes taken during a former year, I begin each year with a new study Bible. I expect a fresh word from God this year and do not need to depend on something He gave me last year.

Choosing a study Bible

It is important that you have a study Bible that you enjoy working in and there are obviously many different ones which will serve nicely. Since 1980, my choice for a study Bible has been the Open Bible Expanded Edition, New King James Version, Thomas Nelson Publishers, Nashville, Tennessee, which is the most complete study Bible for an average Christian that I have found up to this time.

Since I have memorized the King James Version, I am very comfortable with the New King James Version. This version capitalizes pronouns related to Deity, the Holy Spirit, and does a very good job in clarifying passages where language changes over the years make it difficult to get the message from the King James Version. I am constantly amazed at all the study helps in this one volume. There are actually 700 pages of Bible study helps.

In the Open Bible Expanded Edition, the paragraph headings are excellent. The book introductions are thorough, containing an overview, highlighting key verses and chapters in the book, and a working outline. There is information about the author and the time of writing. One feature I particularly appreciate is one which shows where the Lord Jesus Christ is in that book.

The notes are especially helpful covering systematically all the major doctrines of the Bible. Not only is there a full concordance, there is a cyclopedic index which features 7,000 subjects with all Scriptures pertaining to a subject organized under the topic. A definition is provided for the word.

It is important to be willing to make a financial investment in your study Bible since you will have it in your hand on a daily basis spending quality time in it. My study Bible in genuine leather sells for around $90 in a bookstore and is worth every penny.

A reading approach

In choosing a study Bible, one major feature should be paragraph headings for a number of reasons. One is that sometimes a chapter ends in the middle of a paragraph and the paragraph heading alerts you to keep on reading to get the complete thought. The heading can also serve as a stimulus to get your mind in gear as you begin to read.

My suggestion is to use the paragraph headings to **preview** what you are about to read. A good idea is to ask **questions** as you preview and look for answers as you **read**. While you are reading, it is helpful to look away from the page and **state** to yourself the thoughts you are reading. This accelerates learning. Later, **test** yourself to see if you can remember some of the things you have read. This is the **P-Q-R-S-T** method of study designed for reading material. This provokes **meditation** which is the primary goal in reading. By meditating on the Word, you will begin to see things from God's viewpoint as the Holy Spirit brings alive the Scripture you have learned when you need it.

A Christian's Necessary Food

Sometime ago, the Lord led me to write a book entitled *A Christian's Necessary Food*. There are twelve studies on how to get into the Word of God for yourself. Many practical suggestions are provided which will be useful to the serious believer who desires to read and study the Bible. Copies are available through the office in Murfreesboro, Tennessee.

Summary

In the late 80's, a letter was received from a believer on our *Reflector* mailing list expressing appreciation for the paper and commenting on how stimulating the feature was entitled *Notes from My Bible*. She said that she always shared them with her son in college and wondered if they were available in booklet form. When it came time to write books to supplement the teaching shared in a prayer seminar, I decided that one of the first books must be *Notes from My Bible*. The first edition was released in 1994 and contained 350 notes. Hundreds of copies were disseminated and many shared that the notes blessed them. Many notes were used in church bulletins and newsletters.

As we share the second edition of *Notes from My Bible* which contains one-thousand notes, my prayer is that the Holy Spirit will use these words to speak to the hearts of each reader whether it is to give a shock or a charge. In addition to the notes, tributes to my dad and mother-in-law are included, as well as some of my favorite poems.

May each believer be guided by the Holy Spirit to seek a deeper walk with the Lord Jesus Christ more than ever before and that each one will bear fruit for Him. Above all, may the Lord Himself receive all glory and honor from the benefits of the book.

Yours in Calvary love,

J. Gordon Henry
Murfreesboro, Tennessee

NOTES
from
My BIBLE

Note 1. *I have all the time that I need to accomplish all that God intends me to do this day or this year.*

Note 2. *Verse for the year: "But the people who know their God shall be strong and do exploits"* (**Daniel 11:32**).

Note 3. *He who falls into sin is a man, that grieves at sin is a saint, that boasts of sin is a fool. God stands ready to forgive and restore, but you must take the first step.*

Note 4. *There's no better compass to guide my life than the unchanging Word of God.*

Note 5. *Faith is living without scheming.*

Note 6. *The best commentary on the Bible is the Bible.*

Note 7. *As you study the WORD OF GOD you will develop a desire to communicate with the GOD OF THE WORD.*

Note 8. *When Christ is not first, He is last.*

Note 9. *God speaks through the Word, but we must have "ears to hear" which means a willingness to obey.*

Note 10. *Plan a "confrontation" with God every morning. Talk to Him often during the day; meditate on the truths from His Word throughout the day; be willing to change when God points to areas in your life which need changing. Face-to-face with God is the only way to live.*

Note 11. *Feed the fire of prayer with the fuel of God's Word.*

Note 12. *When the world is cold, make it your business to build some fires.*

Note 13. *If you died, leaving nothing behind except your checkbook, appointment calendar, and Bible, what would others conclude about your life?*

Note 14. *He who plants his seed beneath the sod and waits for it to push away the clod, believes in God.*

Note 15. *When I talk, I only repeat what I already know, but when I listen, I learn.*

Note 16. *Life is not a dress rehearsal.*

Note 17. *A Christian should have a heart 25,000 miles in circumference.*

Note 18. *Doing things right is not as important as doing the right things.*

Note 19. *Adversity supplies friction for the match by which God lights the fuse of desire. This is what often leads to prayer!*

Note 20. *It's never right to do the wrong to do the right.*

Note 21. *To reach our destination, it is not enough to be traveling, we must be on the right road headed in the right direction.*

Note 22. *It is possible to be religious, but lost! Check it out in* **Matthew 19:16-26, Luke 18:9-14,** *and* **John 3** .

Note 23. **Psalm 119:11** *does not instruct us to hide the Word away in our notebook, but in our hearts.*

Note 24. *There is something worse than not knowing the will of God, and that's knowing the will of God and not doing it.*

Note 25. *Good use of time is a matter of ordering priorities so that the things of lasting value receive primary consideration.*

Note 26. *The greatest ability in the work of the Lord is availability.*

Note 27. *A person is either a master or slave of the wealth he possesses.*

Note 28. *Anchor yourself to the throne of God. Then spend each day shortening the rope.*

Note 29. *Serving God means serving people.*

Note 30. *Anything short of obedience is disobedience.*

Note 31. *The devil does a lot with blank cartridges. Don't run too soon!*

Note 32. *Every task is a self-portrait of the one who does it.*

Note 33. *Faith honors God; God honors faith.*

Note 34. *My sense of sin is always in proportion to my nearness to God. See **Isaiah 6** for living proof!*

Note 35. *Sure cures for a rundown spiritual battery are meditation in the Scripture and prayer.*

Note 36. *Unless we love and become burdened with concern, we will not intercede.*

Note 37. *One secret in successful praying is to let your gaze be on God and your glance on your problems. Reverse it and you will come from prayer unfulfilled.*

Note 38. *Every spiritual awakening of which there is a record began with prayer.*

Note 39. *If something is best unsaid, leave it there.*

Note 40. *Learn to look at God as first Source, not last resort.*

Note 41. *Only in giving of oneself is enough taken away to make room for receiving more.*

Note 42. *A WORTHY MOTTO FOR LIFE: To Know Him, and to Make Him Known!*

Note 43. *Good, better, best! Never let it rest until your good is better, and your better best.*

Note 44. *CAREFUL: It's easy to fall into using Christian clichés—empty shells—phrases spoken more from habit than from the heart! DANGER!*

Note 45. *There are no exit signs in hell!*

Note 46. *Adoration is just looking at God and loving Him.*

Note 47. *Most of our prayers are centered around the wrong trinity—"me", "myself", and "I".*

Note 48. *No wind is favorable to the sailor who does not know where he is going.*

Note   49. *God does not promise a comfortable journey, only a safe landing.*

Note   50. *Sorrow is a fruit which God never causes to grow on limbs too weak to bear it.*

Note   51. *Never start the day with the face of your soul unwashed.*

Note   52. *If your prayer life is in "neutral" perhaps it is because your heart is "idoling."*

Note   53. *REMEMBER: God's Word never budges an inch.*

Note   54. *You will never break the promises of God by leaning on them.*

Note   55. *Funny thing about love—the more you give it away, the more you have to give.*

Note   56. *Make no appeal until first you kneel. That's the way to serve with zeal. Don't try to serve God before you've seen God each day.*

Note   57. *To make your dreams come true, you have to wake up first.*

Note   58. *My hands need two kinds of exercise: folding (for prayer) and extending (for service).*

Note   59. *Both he who expects little and he who expects much in prayer will receive what he expects.*

Note   60. *Prayer is a relationship, not a recipe.*

Note   61. *You'll be thankful if you are thinkful.*

Note   62. *Thanksgiving is Thanksliving.*

Note   63. *A Christian's prayer life is the measure of his desire to please God.*

Note   64. *Without God, we are inadequate; with Him, we are invincible.*

Note   65. *One man meeting with God can wield more influence than a marching army.*

Note   66. *We are never so high as when we are on our knees.*

Note   67. *Nothing is beyond the scope of prayer which is not beyond the will of God.*

Note 68. *Maintaining a daily, consistent prayer life is HARD WORK.*

Note 69. *He who receives a good turn should never forget it; he who does one should never remember it.*

Note 70. *Worship God in your home every day; in the church every Sunday.*

Note 71. *Love is like the moon; when it does not increase, it decreases.*

Note 72. *We should use every day as carefully as we use our last match.*

Note 73. *Recreation that puts God in second place is Wreckreation.*

Note 74. *The best news the world has ever heard came from a cemetery.*

Note 75. *Christ's resurrection came on Sunday after PASSOVER, also known as EASTER. Easter is observed on the first Sunday after the first full moon following the beginning of Spring on March 21.*

Note 76. *Nobody ever outgrows the Scriptures; the Book widens and deepens as we study through the years.*

Note 77. *Let your speech be better than silence, or be silent.*

Note 78. *Prayer is a golden river at whose brink some die of thirst while others kneel and drink.*

Note 79. *The best form of spiritual exercise is to touch the floor regularly with your knees.*

Note 80. *Genuine faith, like gold, shows its true character when it is tested by fire.*

Note 81. *Meditating about who God is and what He is like helps you love Him more and more.*

Note 82. *Ask God to let you know Him and He will honor your request.* Master **Daniel 11:32.**

Note 83. *The longer one carries a grudge, the heavier it becomes.*

Note 84. *Sin causes a leak in the cup of joy.*

Note 85. *Restful sleep is the reward of a clear conscience.*

Note   86. *There's no greater feeling than to approach each day with a clear conscience.*

Note   87. *The Word of God acts as a cleanser to your mind.*

Note   88. *You have to will to do the will of the Lord in order to know it.*

Note   89. *If you do not want the fruits of sin, stay out of sin's orchards.*

Note   90. *Prayer is never to be   merely a prefix or a suffix.*

Note   91. *Attempt something so impossible that, unless God is in it, it is doomed to failure.*

Note   92. *God will only answer when you come close enough to hear.*

Note   93. *Sin is the greatest of detectives; be sure your sin will find you out.*

Note   94. *Pray like God keeps His Word!*

Note   95. *Saying "yes" to Jesus is saying "no" to the devil.*

Note   96. *David was a man after God's own heart not because he praised the Lord, but because he obeyed the Lord.* See **Acts 13:22.**

Note   97. *Does my daily schedule show that I believe prayer is the secret of victory in spiritual battle? Remember, you will never win the war if you do not know where the battle is being fought.* **Check Ephesians 6:18.**

Note   98. *The less we pray for ourselves, and the more we pray for others, the nearer we approach Christlikeness.*

Note   99. *Reaching God is the chief objective of prayer and the surest way to get to Him is through the name of Christ.*

Note   100. *"Unless we come apart and rest awhile, we may just plain come apart."* **Vance Havner**

Note   101. *In* **Revelation 4:1-2,** *John saw an occupied throne. It is good to know that God has not abdicated yet* *and is still in control.*

Note 102. *Sin may be sweet in the beginning, but it will be bitter in the end.*

Note 103. *Be sure* **Matthew 6:33** *guides your list of "Things to Do Today."*

Note 104. *Worship is the focus of spirit, soul, and body exclusively on the Object of affection—our Lord and God.*

Note 105. *One who walks with the Lord may be lonely on occasion, but never alone.*

Note 106. *"He is no fool who gives what he cannot keep to gain what he cannot lose."* **Jim Eliot**

Note 107. *Repentance is a change of mind based on new evidence which results in a change of direction. I must repent—the Holy Spirit convicts using the Word!*

Note 108. *The Bible is the most important book I will ever read and study.*

Note 109. *The Bible is the only Book whose Author is always present when the book is read.*

Note 110. *"God didn't give us His rules to mend, but to mind."* **John Wesley**

Note 111. *Morality may keep you out of jail, but not out of hell.*

Note 112. *There should be no competition among lighthouses; pray for all Christian workers and ministries.*

Note 113. *Make sure the thing you are living for is worth dying for!*

Note 114. *No matter what your lot is in life, build something on it. There's always room for a service station.*

Note 115. *Nobody has any more time than you have; we all have 168 hours each week.*

Note 116. *Prayer clears the vision, defines duty, sweetens the spirit, and strengthens the resolve.*

Note 117. *Not only was Jesus an intercessor on earth* **(Luke 22:31-32** *praying for Peter), the very heart of our Lord's present ministry in Heaven is intercession* **(Hebrews 7:25; Hebrews 9:24; Romans 8:34).**

Note 118. *All effective praying is nurtured by the written*

Word of God.

Note 119. *Obtain your marching orders for the day early in the morning in the quiet place of prayer.*

Note 120. *Develop the custom of concentrating on God in the first and last waking moment of each day.*

Note 121. *It is easy to acknowledge God with our lips and deny Him with our lives.*

Note 122. *May I do each day's work for Jesus WITH ETERNITY'S VALUES in view!*

Note 123. *Be sure to make friends before you need them. To have good neighbors, be a good neighbor.*

Note 124. *When finite understanding meets infinite WISDOM, the only response is worship and silence.*

Note 125. *One way to overcome your own problems is to help others overcome theirs.*

Note 126. *One cannot live wrong and pray right.*

Note 127. *All real growth in the spiritual life depends on the practice of secret prayer.*

Note 128. *If there be any truer measure of a man than by what he does, it must be what he gives* (**Acts 20:35**)

Note 129. *Every glimpse inside Heaven shows the residents worshipping.*

Note 130. *After worship comes work in prayer.*

Note 131. *If you don't live it, you don't believe it.*

Note 132. *A call to Heaven is toll-free; God is standing by to fellowship with you personally.*

Note 133. *The Word of God is the only foundation strong enough to stand upon in perilous, stormy times.*

Note 134. *Many people use mighty thin thread when mending their ways.*

Note 135. *Before you let your voice be heard for God, let your voice be heard by God.*

Note 136. *Be sure always to remember that God's commandments are His enablements. Therefore, I can do whatever God has told me to do in His Word.*

Note 137. *God rewards those who earnestly seek Him.*

(Hebrews 11:6) *If you're available, tell Him so.*

Note 138. *We must never substitute Christian service for Christian living.*

Note 139. *The child of God who is walking with God is one who is determined to do right and equally determined not to do wrong.*

Note 140. *An important part of praying is a willingness to be part of the answer.*

Note 141. *In the morning, prayer is the key that opens to us the treasures of God's mercies and blessings; in the evening, it is the key that shuts us up under His protection and safeguard.*

Note 142. *Live every moment as if expecting Him to return at any moment.*

Note 143. *When you meet the Lord in Scriptures, you will long to meet Him in prayer.*

Note 144. *Beware of half-truths; you may get hold of the wrong half.*

Note 145. *Too many of us speak twice before we think once.*

Note 146. *America's favorite indoor pastime is letting the chat out of the bag.*

Note 147. *Walking by faith rather than sight—lives are guided by the only One Who sees, knows, and controls the future.*

Note 148. *You can't be a part of the solution, if you're still a part of the problem.*

Note 149. *Don't pray for the hungry to be fed unless you are willing to help provide the bread.*

Note 150. *You can always right a wrong by forgiving it.*

Note 151. *The Bible does not instruct us to live and learn; it exhorts us to learn and live.*

Note 152. *Prayer is measured by its depth, not its length.*

Note 153. *COUNT ON IT! God grants with each burden the strength to bear it—seldom more, never less.*

Note 154. *God does not ask about your ability or your inability—but about your availability.*

Note 155. *The truest test of Christianity is not on the mountain top, but in the valley; not on the day when everything goes right, but on the occasional one when everything goes wrong.*

Note 156. *Be not simply good. Be good for something.*

Note 157. *God loves to destroy worry and doubt, and He does it best when you are on your knees.*

Note 158. *Praise God for anything that drives you to your knees. Problems which get Christians praying do more good than harm.*

Note 159. *We are called to an everlasting preoccupation with God.*

Note 160. *Don't be afraid of praising God too much; the danger is praising Him too little.*

Note 161. *In all Christians, Christ is present; in some Christians, Christ is prominent; but only in a few Christians is Christ preeminent.*

Note 162. *Here on earth we live in a tent—either content or discontent.*

Note 163. *Self is always the last to go. When sin moves out of personality, the likeness of Jesus moves in.*

Note 164. *God was so pleased with His Son, that He wants a whole heaven full of people just like Him.*

Note 165. *Our efficiency without His sufficiency is only deficiency.*

Note 166. *Five minutes of prayer daily adds up to more than thirty hours of talking to God in a year.*

Note 167. *Prayer is faith verbalized—an encounter with the living God. Enough faith to turn to God in prayer is enough faith to have an answer.*

Note 168. *God weighs our gifts in terms of sacrifice, not size.*

Note 169. *Maturity is the ability to carry money without spending it, finish a job without supervision, or bear an injustice without getting even.*

Note 170. *You will never need more than God can supply.*

Note 171. *If you can't cross the street for Jesus, don't worry about crossing the ocean for Jesus.*

Note 172. *Patience strengthens the spirit, sweetens the temper, stifles anger, extinguishes envy, subdues pride, binds the tongue, and tramples upon temptation.*

Note 173. *As we approach God in prayer, our attitude should be to get His mind in the matter— not try to change it.*

Note 174. *A good test of character is the way you treat people who can do nothing for you.*

Note 175. *Prayerless pews make powerless pulpits.*

Note 176. *Read your Bible daily. Prevent truth decay.*

Note 177. *If you are not as close to God as you used to be, don't make a mistake about who moved.*

Note 178. *Talking to people about God is great, but talking to God about people is greater.*

Note 179. *"My theology is now confined to four little words— 'Christ died for me'."* **Charles Spurgeon**

Note 180. *Calvary is God's blood bank for a sin-sick world.*

Note 181. *Many Christians are so heavenly minded that they are no earthly good.*

Note 182. *When Satan puts you in the furnace, remember God has His hand on the thermostat.*

Note 183. *Prayer is like a computer—you only get out of it what you put into it.*

Note 184. *"Be God's [person] in God's place doing God's work in God's way."* **Hudson Taylor**

Note 185. *An unopened Bible is as useless spiritually as an untouched pantry full of goods is useless physically.*

Note 186. *To get a nation back on its feet, we must first get on our knees.* **See 2 Chronicles 7:14.**

Note 187. *The Bible is the story of God's dealings with people just like me.*

Note 188. *Both sin and pride have "I" in the middle.*

Note 189. *There are a thousand ways of pleasing God,*

but not one without faith.

Note 190. *When you have a hard time making ends meet, put God in between!*

Note 191. *Faithfulness in a little thing is never a little thing to God.*

Note 192. *Prayer and meditation on the Word are sure cures for a run-down spiritual battery.*

Note 193. *To be effective God's Word must be in your heart before it is on your lips.*

Note 194. *The more we love the Word of God the more we will love the God of the Word.*

Note 195. *Adoration is a time of meditation on the majesty, the holiness, the grace, the goodness, and the power of God.* **See 1 Chronicles 9:11.**

Note 196. *Develop the attitude of gratitude.*

Note 197. *The first step toward thanking is thinking.*

Note 198. *Christmas caution: Any object or activity that becomes more important than the Lord Jesus Christ is an idol.*

Note 199. *We are judged by what we finish, not by what we start.*

Note 200. *At Christmas it is easy to acknowledge God with our lips and deny Him with our lives.*

Note 201. *Every rainbow reminds us of our promise-keeping God.*

Note 202. *A bad conscience has a good memory.*

Note 203. *"Come, my soul, thy suit prepare. Jesus loves to answer prayer."* **John Newton**

Note 204. *Daily I can pray about what I need to BE what God wants me to BE and DO what God wants me to DO.*

Note 205. *"Prayer does not fit us for greater works; prayer is the greater work."* **Oswald Chambers**

Note 206. *Anyone can* **act** *like a Christian, but it takes a true Christian to* **react** *like one.*

Note 207. *For every assignment in the Christian life, there are corresponding enablements from God. Where God* *leads, He provides.*

Note 208. *The only foundation strong enough to stand upon in perilous times (***2 Timothy 3:1***) is the unmovable Word of God (***Matthew 24:35***).*

Note 209. *There is no better exercise for the human heart than reaching down and lifting someone up.*

Note 210. *A church that has lost compassion is a lost church.* See **Psalm 126:5-6.**

Note 211. *Some Christians have WILL power; some have WON'T power.*

Note 212. *The more we serve Christ, the less we will serve self.*

Note 213. *Worry is like a rocking chair; it gives you something to do, but doesn't get you anywhere.*

Note 214. *Smile awhile and give your frown a rest.*

Note 215. *A believer should not let anything keep him from church services on Sunday which would not keep him from work on Monday.*

Note 216. *Since praise is what we will be doing in Heaven, don't you think we should get in practice down here?*

Note 217. *God is worthy of all worship because of who He is, what He has done, and what He will do.*

Note 218. *Jesus used private places for prayer. Praying in secret will prevent distraction and promote honesty.*

Note 219. *Prayer is the most demanding exercise in the Christian life.*

Note 220. *Prayer is the most neglected responsibility in the Christian life.*

Note 221. *Trusting is really believing that God will do what He says He will do.*

Note 222. *Today is the tomorrow you worried about yesterday.*

Note 223. *Losing a bad temper is over in a minute; so is a shotgun blast.*

Note 224. *It is not what you do that determines what you think about Jesus; it is what you think of Jesus that*

13

determines what you do.

Note 225. *If you did not do yesterday what God wanted you to do, don't waste time today in regret. Just do it.*

Note 226. *A parent leads his child either towards heaven or hell.*

Note 227. *A Christian can never lift the world unless he is above the world.*

Note 228. *When the world is at its worst is the time when the church should be at its best.*

Note 229. *If you are bent on taking a fling in sin, don't forget it always carries a sting.*

Note 230. *For every minute you spend in anger you rob yourself of sixty seconds of happiness.*

Note 231. *The will of God will never lead you where the grace of God cannot keep you.*

Note 232. *What are you doing personally to make our nation a Christian nation?*

Note 233. *The measure of a person's real character is what he would do if he knew he would never be found out.*

Note 234. *A Smile! Something which adds to your face value!*

Note 235. *Look back, and praise Him. Look up, and trust Him. Look around, and serve Him. Look onward, and expect Him.*

Note 236. *Love is a helpless infant that needs assistance and constant nourishing.*

Note 237. *The ability to speak several languages is often an asset; but to be able to hold your tongue is priceless.*

Note 238. *The only people with whom you should try to get even are those who have done you a good turn.*

Note 239. *When a person helps another up a hill, he will find himself nearer the top.*

Note 240. *The best thing to spend on your children is time.*

Note 241. *Obedience belongs to the Christian; results belong to God.*

Note 242. *When it comes to prayer, many Christians need a "faith lifting."*

Note 243. *The deep truths of the Word are best mined with the spade of meditation.*

Note 244. *We realize the strength of the Anchor when we feel the stress of the storm.*

Note 245. *Love for the Author of the Bible is the best preparation for the study of the Bible.*

Note 246. *Our love for God is best seen in our love for others!*

Note 247. *Put God first and He will be with you at the last.*

Note 248. *Wisdom is seeing things from God's perspective.*

Note 249. *Are you right with God? It may be later than you think.*

Note 250. *True worship acknowledges the true worth-ship of God.*

Note 251. *He who runs from God in the morning is not likely to meet Him the rest of the day.*

Note 252. *How confusing when someone gives good advice, but sets a bad example.*

Note 253. *A Christian should never let adversity get him down—except on his knees.*

Note 254. *What you do with Jesus determines where you will be in eternity.*

Note 255. *Jesus gave His all. How much am I giving?*

Note 256. *The safest place in the world is in God's will.*

Note 257. *The fear of God is the beginning of wisdom and knowledge. HAVE I BEGUN YET?*

Note 258. *Plan a face-to-face confrontation with God every day.*

Note 259. The devil is not omniscient, omnipresent, or omnipotent. He is organized, but is perfectly defeated and has no place to stand—unless a Christian gives him that place.

Note 260. *If it's more precious to you than God, you can* *spell it "I-D-O-L."*

Note   261. *If you don't meet God in prayer and the Word, you don't meet God.*

Note   262. *When we work/minister, we work/minister. When we pray, God works/ministers. God can always accomplish more than we can.*

Note   263. *There is no power shortage in Heaven; prayer connects God's children with the power.*

Note   264. *God hears from Heaven, our Headquarters, where all the needed resources and supplies are kept; He never has to put one of His children on backorder!*

Note   265. *The Bible is a Book of principles to be followed and of promises to be claimed.*

Note   266. *O God, prepare me for what you have prepared for me.*

Note   267. *O God, Your sea is so great, and my boat is so small.   My dependence is upon You.*

Note   268. *O Lord, you know how busy I must be this day. If I forget You, don't forget me and remind me of my neglect.*

Note   269. *O Lord, search me and show me if I have made persons, possessions, or activities IDOLS in my life and made You last.*

Note   270. *Looking back—praise Him. Looking ahead— Trust Him. Looking around—serve Him. Looking up— expect Him!*

Note   271. *Feed your faith.   God rewards those who diligently seek Him.* Study **Hebrews 11:6.**

Note   272. *Apathy is the greatest danger to any Christian.*

Note   273. *Look for good in life and you will find it.*

Note   274. *The church with no prayer meeting is like a workshop without power.*

Note   275. *It's all right to have things that money can buy as long as you have things that money cannot buy.*

Note   276. *The angel fetched Peter from the prison; prayer fetched the angel.*

Note 277. *Everything I have beyond nothing is from God.*

Note 278. *Life asks no questions that faith cannot answer as long as the object of the faith is the Lord Jesus Christ.*

Note 279. *An ear without a tear shall seldom hear; often God washes our eyes with tears that we might see.*

Note 280. *God expects His children to expect great things from Him.*

Note 281. *To ask amiss is to have the wrong motive; the correct motive in all praying is that God will receive glory regardless of the answer.* Read **James 4:3.**

Note 282. *It matters not how often your body kneels in prayer unless your inner man (spirit-soul-heart) is kneeling also.*

Note 283. *In prayer, never hurry for God's answer; but when the answer comes, hurry to act!*

Note 284. *Often, we pray for God to bless us; let's not forget that we need to pray to bless God.*

Note 285. *In prayer, it is easy to do all the talking and then "hang-up" before God answers. Slow down! Listen!*

Note 286. *People are lonely because they build walls instead of bridges.*

Note 287. *Kindness is the language that the deaf can hear and the blind can see.*

Note 288. *The best way to keep happiness is to share it.*

Note 289. *A man wrapped up in himself makes a very small package.*

Note 290. *Christ can do wonders with a broken heart if given all the pieces.*

Note 291. *Bloom where you are planted.*

Note 292. *It takes both rain and sunshine to make a rainbow.*

Note 293. *God will supply, but we must apply.*

Note 294. *Nothing is opened by mistake more than the mouth.*

Note 295. *Habits are first cobwebs, then cables.*

Note 296. *Faith is simply believing that God will do what He said He would do. It is not sense, nor sight, nor reason, but taking God at His Word.*

Note 297. *Faith is confidence in God's faithfulness to me in an uncertain world, on an uncharted course through an unknown future.*

Note 298. *Anger at sin is a sign of spiritual vitality.*

Note 299. *Faith is not faith in faith itself, but faith in what the Lord Jesus Christ has done for me in His death and resurrection.*

Note 300. *Feed your faith daily by learning and believing His promises given in the written Word of God.*

Note 301. *I know Who holds tomorrow and I know He holds my hand.*

Note 302. *He touched me and made me whole.*

Note 303. *It is no secret what God can do.*

Note 304. *My God is real for I can feel Him in my soul.*

Note 305. *We cannot be channels of blessing if our lives are not free from known sin.*

Note 306. *You'll never get a busy signal in the prayer line to Heaven.*

Note 307. *When you pray, it's better to have a heart without words, than words without heart.*

Note 308. *If your prayers are sluggish—start praising, and see how your words sprout wings.*

Note 309. *Satan doesn't care how much we pray, as long as we don't do it today.*

Note 310. *You may have good grounds to pray, but you must first be on praying ground.*

Note 311. *Bitterness can make a person's life as ineffective as water makes a match and become a barrier in his prayer life.*

Note 312. *God has a solution planned before we even know we have a problem.*

Note 313. *The only way to learn to pray is to pray.*

Note 314. *God tells us to burden Him with whatever*

burdens us.
Note 315. *Prayer will loose many a knot that your fingers cannot untie.*

Note 316. *It is not the greatness of our troubles, but the smallness of our faith that makes us complain.*
Note 317. *Never do what you cannot ask God to bless.*
Note 318. *He who does not forgive others destroys the bridge over which he himself must cross.*
Note 319. *The reward of a task well done is to have done it.*
Note 320. *Some people never look up until they are on their backs.*

Note 321. *If there is no appointed time for prayer, soon there will be no time at all for prayer.*
Note 322. *A believer who studies the Scriptures "hit or miss" will usually "miss" more than he" hits."*
Note 323. *The chain of a mother's prayers can link her child to God.*
Note 324. *When you find yourself wearing a spirit of heaviness, put on the garment of praise.*
Note 325. *The Bible is meant to be bread for our daily use, not cake for special occasions.*

Note 326. *Where God's finger points, God's hand will always make a way.*
Note 327. *Satan laughs at our toil, mocks at our wisdom, but trembles when we pray.*
Note 328. *Prayer is asking for rain, and faith is carrying the umbrella.*
Note 329. *Prayer is like a computer; you can only get out of it what you put into it.*
Note 330. *Prayer is the breath of the soul; without it you will turn blue.*

Note 331. *"One reason sin flourishes is that it is treated like a cream puff instead of a rattlesnake."* **Billy Sunday**
Note 332. *Sin comes as a friend to entice you and then becomes a master to enslave you.*

Note 333. *When you flee from temptation, be sure you do not leave behind a forwarding address.*

Note 334. *There is a biblical balance that makes for a blessing: pray as though everything depends on God, but work as though everything depends on us.*

Note 335. *God never comforts us to make us comfortable; rather, He comforts us to make us comforters. Comfort means encouragement.*

Note 336. *"It is quite easy to TALK the Christian life, but God wants the WALK. We need to WALK the TALK."* **Pastor Royal Blue**

Note 337. *The Cross pays man no compliment unless it be this, that God considered man worth dying for!*

Note 338. *The will of God is your greatest security. First find His will, then do it. The will of God will never lead you where the grace of God cannot keep you.*

Note 339. *The man who is truly wise is truly humble.*

Note 340. *There's no future in living in the past.*

Note 341. *"If you would humble me, ask me about my prayers."* **Charles H. Spurgeon**

Note 342. *I accept God's will for my life, whatever it is, whenever it is revealed, wherever it takes me, once and for all.*

Note 343. *The will of God is one's greatest security. Find this will, then do it as the first priority of your Christian walk and talk.*

Note 344. *Lord, give me the courage to part with what I hold most dear if it separates me from You.*

Note 345. *If the people you trust do not trust the Lord, their judgment may become your judgment. Be careful! It is wise to measure twice— cut once!*

Note 346. *Faith is as simple, and as difficult, as believing that God will do what He said that He would do and that He cares.*

Note 347. *It's impossible for faith to overdraw its account on the Bank of Heaven.*

Note 348. *Faith is like a kite; a contrary wind only raises* *it higher.*

Note 349. *Honor is better than honors* (**1 Samuel 2:30**).

Note 350. *We can be sure that God's commandments are His enablements. A believer can do whatever work God has called him to do.*

Note 351. *"Faith never knows where it is being led, but it loves and knows the One who is leading."* **Oswald Chambers**

Note 352. *"We should have fixed hours for praying, so that if we are engaged in some business, the time itself will remind us of our duty."* **St. Jerome**

Note 353. *"Faith and obedience are bound up in the same bundle. He that obeys God, trusts God; and he that trusts God, obeys God."* **Charles Spurgeon**

Note 354. *"The Lord gets his best soldiers out of the highlands of affliction."* **Charles Spurgeon**

Note 355. *God is great, and therefore, He should be sought; He is good, and therefore, will be found.*

Note 356. *You are what you think more than you think.* Use **Philippians 4:6** as a good verse to guide.

Note 357. *Sow a thought, reap an act. Sow an act, reap a habit. Sow a habit, reap a character. Sow a character, reap a destiny.*

Note 358. *Every person who lives a day without Christ is taking a terrible risk.*

Note 359. *Life is not in the wick, nor in the candle, but in the burning.*

Note 360. *An apology is a good way to have the last word.*

Note 361. *We can trust the Word about the Word because God is the One who gave us the Word through the Holy Spirit—and God is fully trustworthy.*

Note 362. *A person can't "spend" eternity anywhere because eternity never ends! What you do with the Lord Jesus determines where you will be in eternity—either in Heaven or Hell.*

Note 363. *The road to God and Heaven is marked only with "One Way" signs.*

Note 364. *In Christian service, there is never any unemployment.*

Note 365. *There's always a future for the people of God.*

Note 366. *An optimist sees an opportunity in every calamity; a pessimist sees a calamity in every opportunity.*

Note 367. *"Lord, when we are wrong, make us willing to change and when we are right, make us easy to live with."*

Note 368. *It is right to be contented with what you have, but it is never right to be contented with what you are.*

Note 369. *Kindness is much like snow—it beautifies everything it covers.*

Note 370. *Everything that is almost right is always wrong.*

Note 371. *Four things come not back: the spoken word, the spent arrow, the past life, and the neglected opportunity.*

Note 372. *Wise is the person who has learned to let the Word explain the Word! Are you wise?*

Note 373. *"Lord, help me remember that nothing is going to happen to me today that you and I cannot handle together."*

Note 374. *"Lord, teach me not to hold in my heart anything that would break yours."*

Note 375. *You can accomplish more in one hour with God than one lifetime without Him* (**Matthew 19:26**).

Note 376. *The man who sings his own praises always gets the wrong pitch.*

Note 377. *Prayer is the talking part of a relationship—a friend talking to a Friend* (**John 15:15**), *a servant talking to his Master* (**Colossians 3:24**), and *the bride talking to the Bridegroom* (**Romans 7:4**).

Note 378. *Nothing great was ever achieved without enthusiasm.*

Note 379. *Live truth instead of merely professing it* (**James 1:22**).

Note 380. *Education can polish men, but only the blood* *of Christ can cleanse them.*

Note 381. *Christmas is a time for genuine giving, not simply swapping gifts.*

Note 382. *Give yourself with your gift; he who receives it will treasure it always.*

Note 383. *Be sure that Christ is at the top of your CHRISTmas list. What's under the tree for Him in celebration of His birthday?*

Note 384. *We have two ears and only one tongue that we might hear more and speak less.*

Note 385. *Talk may be cheap, but we often pay dearly for it* (**James 3:5**).

Note 386. *"Private place and plenty of time are the life of prayer."* **E. M. Bounds**

Note 387. *When Joseph fled from sexual temptations, he lost his coat, but kept his character.*

Note 388. *"Little faith will take your soul to Heaven, but great faith will bring Heaven to your soul."* **Charles Spurgeon**

Note 389. *The man caught up in this world is not ready for the next one.*

Note 390. *"We do not need more national development, we need more spiritual power. We do not need more knowledge, we need more character."* **Dwight David Eisenhower**

Note 391. *While in this life, a Christian is never in a state of completion, but in the process of becoming.*

Note 392. *Instead of putting others in their place, put yourself in their place.*

Note 393. *What I know of God encourages me to trust Him in all I do not know.*

Note 394. *Our prayer and God's mercy are like two buckets in a well; while one ascends, the other descends.*

Note 395. *To fail to learn from failure is to ensure future failures.*

Note 396. *A believer's highest aspiration should be "Thy*

23

will be done"—*nothing more, nothing less, nothing else* (**Matthew 26:42**).

Note 397. *Theodore Roosevelt noted that the only book Abraham Lincoln ever mastered was the Bible. After a certain point, every address Lincoln gave was permeated with the Word of God.*

Note 398. *A Christian must keep the faith—but not to himself.*

Note 399. *A friend loves at all times—not on again and off again.*

Note 400. *Count on it! A friend steps in even when the whole world steps out.*

Note 401. *A good leader is one who knows the way, shows the way, and goes the way.*

Note 402. *A good marriage is the union of two forgivers.*

Note 403. *A harvest does not come without the planting of seed.*

Note 404. *A healthy fear of Hell has sent many a soul to Heaven.*

Note 405. *A little sin will add to your trouble, subtract from your energy, and multiply your difficulties.*

Note 406. *A man may go to Heaven without wealth, health, riches, honor, learning, or friends; but he can never go to Heaven without Christ.*

Note 407. *A person too big to be willing to do little things is too little to be trusted with big things in God's economy.*

Note 408. *A pint of example is worth a gallon of advice.*

Note 409. *A religion that cost nothing is worth nothing. Faith which refuses to pay the price is spurious faith.*

Note 410. *A smooth sea never made a skillful sailor.*

Note 411. *Although the tongue weighs very little, few people are able to hold it.*

Note 412. *Apply yourself wholly to the Scriptures and the Scriptures wholly to yourself.*

Note 413. *As a man grows older and wiser, he talks less and says more.*

Note 414. *A real friend makes a difference: "As iron*

sharpens iron, so a man sharpens the countenance of his friend" (**Proverbs 27:17**).

Note 415. *The only way to ponder properly the meaning of Christmas is to go back to the first one.*

Note 416. *At Bethlehem, long ago, God demonstrated that to love is to give one's best.*

Note 417. *Bad habits are like a comfortable bed—easy to get into at night, but hard to get out of in the morning!*

Note 418. *Be careful of your private thoughts; they may break forth into actions at anytime.*

Note 419. *Be holy for God and He will be wholly for you.*

Note 420. *Be humble, or you'll surely stumble.*

Note 421. *Be patient with the faults of others; they have to be patient with yours.*

Note 422. *Begin the day with Christ, your Lord; kneel down to Him in prayer. Lift up your head to His abode, and get your orders there.*

Note 423. *Believers at war with their brothers cannot be at peace with their Father.*

Note 424. *Better to look ahead and prepare than to look back and despair.*

Note 425. *Better to pay the price of obedience than the penalty of disobedience.*

Note 426. *Bless the Lord today; He blesses you every day.*

Note 427. *Careful meditation on the Scriptures makes for a closer walk with the Savior along life's highway.*

Note 428. *Christ became a curse for us to remove the curse from us—Amazing love!*

Note 429. *Christ died for us that we might live for Him! It's that simple!*

Note 430. *Christlikeness is best developed in the darkroom of prayer.*

Note 431. *Christ reigning WITHIN is the explanation for victory over the world WITHOUT.*

Note 432. *Christ was delivered FOR our sins that we might be delivered FROM our sins.*

Note 433. *Christ who tells us of Heaven with all its happiness also tells us of Hell with all its horrors.*

Note 434. *Sin for the Christian has two aspects—doing forbidden things (commission) and failing to do expected things (omission).*

Note 435. *Christianity worth having is worth sharing.*

Note 436. *Christians will do well to remove from their memories the sins which God has erased from their record and from His own memory.*

Note 437. *"Christ's second coming is the perpetual light on the path which makes the present bearable."* **G. Campbell Morgan**

Note 438. *Conscience is like a pencil. It works best after being sharpened by God's Word.*

Note 439. *Death for the Christian is a glorious beginning, not an ending; a wondrous arriving, not a departing.*

Note 440. *Discontentment makes rich men poor while contentment makes poor men rich.*

Note 441. *Discretion of speech is better than fluency.*

Note 442. *Do not have your daily concert before you tune your instruments. Begin the day with God.*

Note 443. *Do what you can where you are with what you have which is all God expects* (**Galatians 6:10**).

Note 444. *Do your work as unto the Lord. The pay may not be much, but the retirement plan is out of this world.*

Note 445. *Don't expect to lead to Christ souls you do not love.*

Note 446. *Don't let religious rituals keep you from getting to know God and His Word better.*

Note 447. *Every temptation is an opportunity to flee to God.*

Note 448. *Everybody's business is usually nobody's business.*

Note 449. *Example is a language everybody can read—young and old!*

Note 450. *Failure to do right is just as sinful as doing wrong.*

Note 451. *Faith is basically obedience to the commands of God.*

Note 452. *Faith is the hand that must take God's gift.*

Note 453. *Faith will fold unless it feeds on the promises of God's written Word.*

Note 454. *Gentle words fall lightly, but have great weight.*

Note 455. *Give according to your income lest God makes your income according to your giving.*

Note 456. *Give your all to Christ; He gave His all for you.*

Note 457. *Giving is the thermometer which registers our love.*

Note 458. *God can take the place of anything, but nothing can take the place of God.*

Note 459. *God gives us the freedom to choose how to use His gifts, but holds us responsible for our choices.*

Note 460. *"God is not only loving, He is also just; therefore, every sin must be pardoned or punished."* **William Booth**

Note 461. *God will never ask us to go where He will not lead.*

Note 462. *God doesn't keep office hours; nor does He put a secretary between himself and a believer.*

Note 463. *God formed us; sin deformed us; Christ transforms us (2 Corinthians 5:17).*

Note 464. *God has you in His plans and in His mind; do you have Him in yours?*

Note 465. *"God loves everyone of us as though there was but one of us to love."* **Augustine**

Note 466. *"God makes no mistakes. The stops of a good man are ordered as well as his steps."* **George Mueller**

Note 467. *Yesterday—He loved me! Today—He's just the same! How long will this continue? Forever! Praise*

His name.

Note 468. *You can expect God to intervene when you have taken time to intercede.*

Note 469. *God sees the heart, not the hand—the giver, not the gift.*

Note 470. *God wants to be in total control of all that we are and all that we do.*

Note 471. *God writes with a pen that never blots, speaks with a tongue that never slips, and acts with a hand that never fails.*

Note 472. *God's children never part for the last time.*

Note 473. *God's giving deserves our thanksgiving* **(Psalm 68:19).**

Note 474. *God's grace can save the best of sinners as well as the worst of sinners.*

Note 475. *God's help is only a prayer away.*

Note 476. *God's love does not exempt us from trials, but it does see us through them.*

Note 477. *God's Spirit is your power source, but even a little sin can break the connection.*

Note 478. *God's Word is like a life preserver; it keeps the soul from sinking in the sea of trouble.*

Note 479. *God's words tell us of His love; our words should tell Him of our love.*

Note 480. *Guard against the pervasive sin of vindictiveness and let Him correct all wrongs against us.*

Note 481. *Habit is much like a cable. Weave a thread each day and at last you cannot break it.*

Note 482. *Harken to the "come" of salvation's invitation and you will never hear the "depart" of damnation at the end of life's journey.*

Note 483. *He that loves reading has everything within his reach.*

Note 484. *He understands when men misunderstand.*

Note 485. *God never closes one door that He doesn't open another.*

Note 486. *He who finds no fault in himself needs a second opinion.*

Note 487. *He who is on the road to Heaven should not be content to go there alone.*

Note 488. *He who overcomes his own anger overcomes a strong enemy.*

Note 489. *He who plants weeds must not expect to gather flowers.*

Note 490. *"He who spreads the sails of prayer will eventually fly the flag of praise."* **Charles Spurgeon**

Note 491. *He who would spend time wisely must learn to invest it in eternity.*

Note 492. *Heaven is a prepared place for prepared people.*

Note 493. *Helping someone who can never return the favor in the name of the Lord Jesus Christ is showing real love.*

Note 494. *"His promises are checks to be cashed, not mere mottoes to hang on the wall."* **Vance Havner**

Note 495. *Honest restitution is a mark of genuine repentance.*

Note 496. *Honesty does not have degrees.*

Note 497. *Honesty is the best policy.*

Note 498. *How can I be content to give so little when Christ gives so much?*

Note 499. *Humans were made to run on love, and they do not function well on anything else.*

Note 500. *Hurry is the mother of many mistakes.*

Note 501. *A good example is the best sermon.*

Note 502. *If you are a stranger to prayer, you are a stranger to power.*

Note 503. *"If you don't want to trade with the devil, stay out of his shop."* **Vance Havner**

Note 504. *If you have accomplished all that you planned for your life, you have not planned enough.*

Note 505. *If your light is shining for Jesus, God will put it where it can be seen.*

Note 506. *If you think God makes mistakes, you are mistaken!*

Note 507. *If we cannot do the good we would, we ought to do the good we can.*

Note 508. *God is with you and there is nothing like His presence to shed new light on any dark situation.*

Note 509. *If you're in step with the world, you're out of step with God.*

Note 510. *"I'm just a NOBODY telling EVERYBODY about SOMEBODY who can save ANYBODY—who turns to the SOMEBODY, the Lord Jesus Christ, in faith and trust!"* **A Converted Alcoholic**

Note 511. *"In all literature, there is nothing which compares with the Bible."* **John Milton**

Note 512. *In company, guard your tongue; in solitude, your thoughts.*

Note 513. *In God's works we see His hand, but in His Word, we see His heart.*

Note 514. *Instead of criticizing the Bible, God's Word, let the Bible criticize you.*

Note 515. *It is better to beg for bread on earth than to beg for water in hell* (**Luke 16**).

Note 516. *It is easy to sing when we walk with the King.*

Note 517. *"It is impossible to rightly govern the world without God and the Bible."* **George Washington**

Note 518. *It is well to remember that ANGER is just one letter short of DANGER.*

Note 519. *"It takes less time to do things right than it does to explain why you did it wrong."* **Henry Wadsworth Longfellow**

Note 520. *It takes a real storm to prove the real shelter.*

Note 521. *It takes two sides to make a lasting peace, but it only takes one to make the first step.*

Note 522. *It's a good idea to tune your instrument by prayer before the concert of the day begins.*

Note 523. *It's a great thing to do a little thing well.*

Note 524. *It's always too soon to quit!*

Note 525. *It's important for faith to draw from its account in the Bank of Heaven.*

Note 526. *It's never too early to accept Christ, but at any moment it could be too late (2 Corinthians 6:2).*

Note 527. *It's not the hours you put in, but what you put into the hours, that counts.*

Note 528. *Jesus came into the world to talk to men for God; now, He is in Heaven to talk to God for men.*

Note 529. *Jesus came into the world to save the last and the least.*

Note 530. *Jesus Christ is the Light that never has a power failure.*

Note 531. *Keep praying, but be thankful that God's answers are always wiser than our praying.*

Note 532. *Keep your heart right, even when it is sorely wounded.*

Note 533. *Kindness is life's sunshine.*

Note 534. *Kindness is the oil that takes the friction out of life.*

Note 535. *Kneeling in prayer keeps you in good standing with God.*

Note 536. *Knowing the Living Word (the Lord Jesus Christ) is the key that unlocks the truths of the written Word (the Bible).*

Note 537. *Lay hold on the Bible until the Bible lays hold on you.*

Note 538. *Let no picture hang on the walls of your imagination that you would not allow to hang on the walls of your home.*

Note 539. *God's part we cannot do; our part, He will not do.*

Note 540. *Little is much when God is in it.*

Note 541. *Live for Christ; He died for you.*

Note 542. *Live the Gospel first; tell others about it afterwards.*

Note 543. *Living without Christ means dying without*

31

hope.

Note 544. *Living without God is like driving in heavy fog.*

Note 545. *Losing your temper is no way to get rid of it.*

Note 546. *Love for God is evidenced by our love for others.*

Note 547. *Love is never afraid of giving too much.*

Note 548. *Love is the Christian's ID card.*

Note 549. *Man knows no want when the Lord is His supply.*

Note 550. *Man's requirements are no drain on God's resources.*

Note 551. *"Man's soul finds no rest until it rests in God."* **Augustine**

Note 552. *Many Christians who pray "our Father" on Sunday act like orphans the rest of the week.*

Note 553. *Men of the Word should be men of their word.*

Note 554. *Mercy keeps us from getting what we deserve; grace gives us what we don't deserve.*

Note 555. *Morning prayers lead to evening praises.*

Note 556. *Neglecting the Word will famish your soul; memorizing the Word will feed it* (**Psalm 119:11**).

Note 557. *No person outgrows Scriptures; the Book widens and deepens with use year by year for the one who reads it drinking at God's fountain of knowledge.*

Note 558. *No weapon in Satan's arsenal can destroy the Sword of the Spirit, which is the Word of God.*

Note 559. *Nothing but the Bread of Life can satisfy spiritual hunger* (**John 6:35**).

Note 560. *Nothing sets a person out of the devil's reach as much as genuine humility.*

Note 561. *"O God, I have tested Thy goodness and it both satisfied me and made me thirsty for more."* **A. W. Tozer**

Note 562. *Of all the things you wear, your expression is the most important.*

Note 563. *One reason the School of Experience is so tough is that you get the test first and the lesson later.*
Note 564. *One thing you can give and still keep is your word.*
Note 565. *One who worships God participates in the chief occupation of Heaven.*

Note 566. *When you feel like running away, run to God.*
Note 567. *Our greatest gift to others is a good example for them to model.*
Note 568. *Our sense of sin is always in proportion to our nearness to God.*
Note 569. *Outside the will of God, there can be no true success; in the will of God, there can be no failure.*
Note 570. *Patience is a virtue that carries a lot of wait.*

Note 571. *Pause to think and you will find cause to thank.*
Note 572. *People's minds are like parachutes; to function properly, they must first open.*
Note 573. *Plan your work; work your plan.*
Note 574. *Prayer can do anything that God can do.*
Note 575. *Prayer includes listening to what God might want to say to you—not just talking to Him.*

Note 576. *Prayer is His child's call to the Father's ear, the Father's heart, and the Father's ability.*
Note 577. *Prayer is the highest use to which speech can be put; we must never abuse it.*
Note 578. *Prayer will drive out sin in your life, or sin will drive out prayer.*
Note 579. *Prayer's prevailing power puts omnipotence into operation; God moves when His children pray.*
Note 580. *Procrastination has never landed one soul in Heaven, but it has doomed many to an eternal Hell.*

Note 581. *Procrastination is the thief of time* (**Psalm 90:12**).
Note 582. *Promises of God are not mere mottoes to hang on the wall, but checks to be cashed.*
Note 583. *Resurrection is a keystone of Christian faith*

and biblical revelation; the resurrection is the Father's "Amen" to our Lord's cry from the Cross, "It is finished!"

Note 584. *Put your burden on the Lord; if you will do the CASTING, He will do the CARING* (**1 Peter 5:6-7**).

Note 585. *Safety does not consist in the absence of danger, but in the presence of God.*

Note 586. *Salvation is not something we achieve, but something we receive.*

Note 587. *"Satan is the accuser of the brethren. Let's leave the dirty work to him!"* **Harry Ironside**

Note 588. *Satan is to be avoided as a lion, dreaded as a serpent, but most to be feared, as an angel of light.*

Note 589. *Satan laughs at our powers, mocks at our wisdom, but trembles at God's Word.*

Note 590. *So live that when people get to know you, they will know Christ better.*

Note 591. *Some make others happy wherever they go; others whenever they go. What about you?*

Note 592. *Some who expect to be saved at the eleventh hour, die at ten-thirty.*

Note 593. *Staying calm is the best way to take the wind out of any angry man's sail.*

Note 594. *Strive to develop the attitude of gratitude.*

Note 595. *Strong drink produces weak character.*

Note 596. *Study the Bible to be wise; believe it to be safe; practice it to be holy.*

Note 597. *The "best flings" in life are never free!*

Note 598. *The best way to remember people is in prayer.*

Note 599. *The best way to stay young is to keep active serving God and others totally.*

Note 600. *The Bible is like a compass—it always points the believer in the right direction.*

Note 601. *"The 'blessed hope' is Heaven's balm for earthly sorrow"* (**2 Thessalonians 3:5**). **Charles Spurgeon**

Note 602. *The cure for nearsighted vision is farsighted* *prayer.*

Note 603. *The greatest of all mistakes is to do nothing because you think you can do only a little.*

Note 604. *The hand that gives—gathers!*

Note 605. *The ladder of hope has nothing to stand on here below; it is held up from above.*

Note 606. *The nail-pierced hands of Jesus reveal the love-filled heart of God.*

Note 607. *The man who only samples God's Word occasionally will never acquire much of a taste for it.*

Note 608. *The meat of the Word is most nourishing when combined with the daily exercise of obedience.*

Note 609. *The more you love Christ, the more you will be homesick for Heaven.*

Note 610. *The more we die to self, the more we live to God.*

Note 611. *The most deadly sins do not leap upon us; they creep upon us.*

Note 612. *The most expensive thing in the world is sin for it may cost you your soul.*

Note 613. *The most likable people are those who are most like Christ.*

Note 614. *The most important part of Christmas is the first six letters.*

Note 615. *A Christian may come to the end of his rope, but never to the end of his hope.*

Note 616. *The number of times some say "no" to temptation is once weakly.*

Note 617. *The One who died as our Substitute on the Cross now lives as our Advocate at the right hand of the Father.*

Note 618. *The only time it's not a sin to get angry is when you get angry at sin.*

Note 619. *The only valid passport to Heaven is signed in Jesus' blood.*

Note 620. *The person who looks up to God rarely looks down on others.*

Note 621. *A successful relationship with God counts for eternity; everything else is perishable.*

Note 622. *The sign on God's Highway may read WINDING ROAD—but it points the way Home to Heaven.*

Note 623. *The Son of God became the Son of Man so that sons of men might become sons of God.*

Note 624. *The surest way to make it hard for your children is to make it soft for them.*

Note 625. *The truth of a matter is not determined by how many people believe it.*

Note 626. *The truths and promises of Scripture may be compared to fragrant flowers; meditation, like the bee, sucks the honey out of them.*

Note 627. *The way of obedience is the way of blessing.*

Note 628. *The world at its worse requires a Christian at his best.*

Note 629. *There are no accidents with God.*

Note 630. *There are three answers to prayer: yes, no, and wait awhile.*

Note 631. *There is a bank account in our name in Heaven's Bank. We ought to use our* **checkbook of faith and prayer.**

Note 632. *There is a difference between the many books men make and the one Book that makes men.*

Note 633. *There is no reward from God to those who seek it from man.*

Note 634. *There is nothing around the corner that is beyond God's view.*

Note 635. *These two are wedded and no man can part— dust on the Bible and drought in the heart.*

Note 636. *They witness best whose WALK squares with their TALK.*

Note 637. *Those who start telling little white lies will soon go colorblind* (**Colossians 3:9**).

Note 638. *"Thou art coming to a King, large petitions with thee bring; For His grace and power are such, none can* *ever ask too much."* **John Newton**

Note 639. *To be rich in God is better than to be rich in earthly goods.*

Note 640. *To wait on the Lord is to put your weight on His promises.*

Note 641. *Today's preparation determines tomorrow's achievement.*

Note 642. *Too many persons are in too much of a hurry going in too many directions to nowhere for nothing.*

Note 643. *Treasures in Heaven are laid up as treasures on earth are laid down.*

Note 644. *True freedom is found only in bondage to Christ.*

Note 645. *Turning the other cheek often turns others to Christ.*

Note 646. *Unless we see the CROSS overshadowing the CRADLE, we've missed the real meaning of Christmas.*

Note 647. *Unless your finger is clean, don't point it toward others.*

Note 648. *Waste not—want not.*

Note 649. *We are not cisterns made for storing, but channels made for sharing.*

Note 650. *We are not to be terminals of God's gifts to us; we are intended to be channels through whom the blessings can flow to others.*

Note 651. *We do our best kneeling when we are in good standing with God.*

Note 652. *We don't need more to be thankful for; we need to be more thankful for what we have* (**Psalm 100:4**).

Note 653. *We lie to God in prayer when we don't rely on Him after prayer.*

Note 654. *We make our decisions, and our decisions then make us.*

Note 655. *We must know His GRACE here in order to see His FACE in Heaven.*

Note 656. *When a sermon pricks your conscience, it must* have had some sharp points.

Note 657. *When fear knocks at your door, send faith to answer it and you'll find no one is there.*

Note 658. *When God is going to do something wonderful, He often begins with a difficulty.*

Note 659. *When looking for "secret faults," remember you can begin at either end of SIN and find "I" in the middle.*

Note 660. *You can give without loving, but you can't love without giving.*

Note 661. *The Christian's future is as bright as the promises of God and his willingness to claim the promises.*

Note 662. *When we bend our knees in prayer, God bends His ear to listen.*

Note 663. *When we get to the place where there's nothing left but God, we find that God is enough.*

Note 664. *When you are swept off your feet, slip down on your knees.*

Note 665. *When you see a worthy person, emulate him; when you see an unworthy person, examine yourself.*

Note 666. *When you see someone without a smile, give him one of yours.*

Note 667. *Worry does not empty tomorrow of its sorrow, it empties today of its strength.*

Note 668. *Where the Lord puts a period, don't change it to a question mark.*

Note 669. *When you want others to know what Christ will do for them, let them see what Christ has done for you.*

Note 670. *While the Christian must live in the world, he should not allow the world to live in Him.*

Note 671. *Witnessing is more than what we say, it's what we are.*

Note 672. *Woman—last at the Cross and first at the grave!*

Note 673. *Worldly investments will never pay eternal dividends.*

Note 674. *Worry is a burden Christians were never meant* *to bear.*

Note 675. *Worry is unbelief parading in disguise and pulls tomorrow's clouds over today's sunshine.*

Note 676. *Would you want Christ to represent you above in the same way that you represent Him below?*

Note 677. *"You can make more friends in two months by becoming interested in other people than you can in two years by trying to get other people interested in you."* **Dale Carnegie**

Note 678. *You can never break God's promises by leaning on them.*

Note 679. *You can never do a kindness too soon, for you never know how soon it will be too late.*

Note 680. *You can never speak to the wrong person about Christ.*

Note 681. *You can often tell a wise man by the things he doesn't say.*

Note 682. *You can't take your wealth with you, but Christ said you can send it on ahead* (**Matthew 6:19**).

Note 683. *You can't really GIVE thanks until you LIVE thanks.*

Note 684. *You lack holiness within if you can't blush at sin.*

Note 685. *You can depend upon the Lord; can the Lord depend on you?*

Note 686. *"A fire kindled against an enemy often burns you more than him."* **Chinese Proverb**

Note 687. *Effectual prayer does not require eloquence, but it does require earnestness.*

Note 688. *God and prayer go together; to neglect one is to neglect the other.*

Note 689. *God measures how much we love Him by how much we love others* (**Matthew 5:46**).

Note 690. *God often begins mighty works through one person; the principle is getting fire started with kindling wood.*

Note 691. *God often uses small matches to light great torches.*

Note 692. *If you have no room for Jesus in your heart now, there'll be no room in Heaven for you later.*

Note 693. *"O how blessed is the promise When our spirit is set free: To be absent from the body Means to live, O Lord, with Thee."* **Matthew Henry**

Note 694. *"Pray as if everything depends on God, then work as if everything depends on you."* **Martin Luther**

Note 695. *Prayer should be the key with which you open the gates of day and close the door of night.*

Note 696. *Reach up as far as you can by faith; trust God to do the rest.*

Note 697. *To master yourself, give yourself to the Master* **(Proverbs 25:28).**

Note 698. *When Satan attacks, submit yourself to God and strike back with the Sword of the Spirit, which is the Word of God* **(James 4:7).**

Note 699. *When the prayer of faith goes to market, it always takes a basket.*

Note 700. *Where love is thin, faults are thick!*

Note 701. *A Christian does not have to be defeated; Satan has no place to stand unless he is given a place* **(Ephesians 4:27).**

Note 702. *A clear conscience—one devoid of a desire for sin—is necessary for effective praying* **(Hebrews 10:22, 1 John 3:21).**

Note 703. *A gossip is a person with a wrong sense of rumor.*

Note 704. *A "yes, Lord" attitude is submission and obedience to do what He wants you to do before you know what it is; it makes no room for the veto power which is administered after you know His will.*

Note 705. *Adoration is looking at God and loving Him for who He is.*

Note 706. *All elements of prayer*—adoration, confession, thanksgiving, petition, intercession—*presuppose a sense of* *need.*

Note 707. *All you need to know to be content is this: God is good.*

Note 708. *Anyone can obey God when the task is easy and everyone behind it; faith obeys when the task seems impossible and others oppose it.*

Note 709. *As you genuinely confess your sins, God takes them away* (**John 1:29**), *forgets them* (**Hebrews 10:17**), *washes them away* (**Isaiah 1:18**), *blots them out* (**Isaiah 43:25**), *wipes them out like a cloud* (**Isaiah 44:2**), *pardons them* (**Isaiah 55:7**), *and buries them into the depths of the sea* (**Micah 7:19**).

Note 710. *Ask God to conduct a full-scale investigation in your life in order to keep the prayer channel clear and open* (**Psalm 139:23-24**).

Note 711. *Ask God to show you sins in your life and make a sin list to use for repentance and confession.*

Note 712. *Big problems put a Christian into a perfect position to watch God give big answers as He exercises His great power on our behalf.*

Note 713. *Buckpassing is like trying to throw away a boomerang; it always comes back to hit you.*

Note 714. *Burnout comes when we begin to look at work first.*

Note 715. *"By prayer we enter into God's holy temple, and penetrate at once to the throne of grace. Prayer is not only the shortest distance to God's mighty throne, it is the only way in. To think that this supreme wonder could take place so suddenly with one bold, blood-bought step! There we see the Lord Jesus ever living to pray for us, and ready to give us of His own praying by His Spirit. Glorious discovery. HE IS ONLY A PRAYER AWAY! The veil of sense and space that hides Him within His temple-universe is suddenly removed as we pray. We enter silently into His temple, and lo, suddenly we are before His throne. Priests, before our great High Priest. There, too, we are suddenly in the presence of angels and archangels, and with all the company of Heaven we worship and adore Him. Only there do we discover the wonder of worship, that worship is* *before work, and that all His works are done in the spirit of worship. There are many churchgoers, but few worshipers, because there are few pray-ers!"* **Armin R. Gesswein**

Note 716. *Careful! Don't toss a few clichés to God and call it prayer.*

Note 717. *Confession is agreeing with God about sin and saying the same thing that He says about specific sin in our lives.*

Note 718. *Confession is my response to the holiness of God* (**Psalm 51:1, Hebrews 4:16**).

Note 719. *Darkness is vanquished by the presence of Light.*

Note 720. *Establish a time to meet the Lord each day since people seldom do things to any degree of regularity who don't do them at a set time.*

Note 721. *God can strike some mighty strong licks with a crooked stick. Remember Jonah? He can use us all!*

Note 722. *God does not ask us to go where He has not provided the means to help.*

Note 723. *God feeds the birds, but He does not put the worms in their nests.*

Note 724. *God is the only one in a position to look down on others, so don't you try it.*

Note 725. *God specializes in things thought impossible and can do what no other can do.*

Note 726. *God works only in concert with the praying of His people.*

Note 727. *God's heart's desire is that no person perish, but that each one come to repentance* (**2 Peter 3:9**).

Note 728. *He who is "born of God" should increasingly resemble his Father.*

Note 729. *You can turn any care into prayer anywhere.*

Note 730. *If I don't talk to God, it is an indication that He is really playing a secondary role in my life, and as a result I will never be the person God wants me to be.*

Note 731. *If sin is against another person, confess it to*

God, and make things right with the person.
Note 732. *If sin is against God, confess it to God, and make things right with God.*
Note 733. *If sin is against a group, confess it to God, and make things right with the group.*
Note 734. *If you are not praying for members of your family, you can be sure that no one else is.*
Note 735. *If you are not willing to establish an appointment with God on a daily basis, you are unlikely to become a prayer warrior.*

Note 736. *If your plans are only to pray when you get around to it, the devil will see you never get around to it.*
Note 737. *In prayer, the Holy Spirit activates the Word of God which we have put into our minds by reading, hearing, studying, and memorizing.*
Note 738. *Intercession is my response to God's love for all people.*
Note 739. *It is better to look ahead and prepare than to look back and regret.*
Note 740. *It won't matter when you get to the top of the ladder of success if your ladder is leaning against the wrong building.*

Note 741. *Jesus! Don't leave earth without Him!*
Note 742. *"Jesus Christ is not valued at all until He is valued above all."* **Augustine**
Note 743. *Let your first objective be simply to read your Bible to know God better and experience the joy of His presence.*
Note 744. *Life is fragile! Handle with prayer!*
Note 745. *"Lord, You be the needle and I will be the thread. You go first and I will follow wherever You lead."* **Congolese Convert**

Note 746. *God's time to act is never too early or too late.*
Note 747. *Meaningful encounter with the Lord requires time when the total person—spirit, soul, body—exclusively devotes attention toward Him without distraction.*
Note 748. *Memories that are not constantly refreshed will*

quickly recede. God gave us a MEMORY that we might have roses in the winter and we should use it!

Note 749. *Most Christians do not do enough work—spending energy—in prayer in a year to make a butterfly tired!*

Note 750. *No sin is too small to hinder our fellowship with God.*

Note 751. *On Judgment Day, each of us will stand alone, accountable before God.*

Note 752. *Only God deserves our complete loyalty and obedience.*

Note 753. *Pause, during your praying, to listen to God's voice in your spirit* (**Psalm 62:5, Psalm 46:10**).

Note 754. *Plan a daily confrontation with God when you talk to Him and meditate on His truths, gleaned from His Word, throughout the day. When He points to areas in your life that are not pleasing to Him, be willing to change.*

Note 755. *Praise and thanksgiving must be expressed to be valid* (**Psalm 30:11-12, 107:2**).

Note 756. *Praise and thanksgiving please the heart of God* (**Psalm 22:3, Hebrews 13:15-16**).

Note 757. *Praise doesn't change God; He will never be any greater than He already is. Instead, praise changes us and causes us to want to walk with Him.*

Note 758. *Praise is a powerful weapon and renders Satan helpless in its midst—for God inhabits the praises of His people* (**Psalm 22:3**).

Note 759. *Prayer and Bible study go hand in hand, for there is no true prayer independent of God's written Word.*

Note 760. *Throw mud and you will have dirty hands, whether or not the mud hits the mark.*

Note 761. *Prayer is entering into God's Throne Room any hour of the day or night. You don't have to have prior appointment since God is always there. He doesn't keep office hours. He not only wants you to come, you can stay as long as you want to stay when you get there. There is no time limit.*

Note 762. *Prayer is my response to God's invitation to come to Him for wisdom* (**James 1:5**).

Note 763. *Prayer is my response to God's invitation to fellowship* (**Psalm 27:4, 8**).

Note 764. *Prayer is my response to the character of God—who He is—His person, presence, position, power, greatness, majesty, and His love* (**Psalm 145:3**).

Note 765. *Prayer is my response to the invitation of God to cast all my cares on Him* (**1 Peter 5:7**).

Note 766. *"Prayer is not the foe of work; it does not paralyze activity. It works mightily; prayer itself is the greatest work."* **E. M. Bounds**

Note 767. *Prayer is reporting to duty.*

Note 768. *Prayer is the gymnasium of the soul.*

Note 769. *Prayer is the talking part of a relationship and verbal communication is necessary for healthy relationships.*

Note 770. *Prayer must mean something to us if it is to mean anything to God.*

Note 771. *Prayer reveals God and is my response to who He is.*

Note 772. *Prayer without faith is a farce.*

Note 773. *Prayerlessness is more than an area of neglect or an area of regret, it is sin* (**1 Samuel 12:23**).

Note 774. *Read your Bible with a pen or pencil in hand to be ready for His message.*

Note 775. *Rearing children is like drafting a blueprint; you have to know where to draw the line.*

Note 776. *Salvation is free, but discipleship is costly.*

Note 777. *Satan can't counterfeit genuine prayer.*

Note 778. *Watch your thoughts, they become words. Watch your words, they become actions. Watch your actions, they become habits. Watch your habits, they become your character. Watch your character, it becomes your destiny.*

Note 779. *Self-sufficiency is the attitude that closes the door to God's mercy.*

Note 780. *You cannot truly help men by doing for them*

what they could and should do for themselves.

Note 781. *Since God is greater than any circumstance or situation we are in, we can give Him praise even in the midst of trouble.*

Note 782. *Thank God every day for one material blessing and tell Him why you are thankful.*

Note 783. *Thank God every day for one person in your life and tell Him why you are thankful.*

Note 784. *Thank God every day for one physical blessing and tell Him why are are thankful.*

Note 785. *Thank God every day for one spiritual blessing and tell Him why you are thankful.*

Note 786. *Tell your children and grandchildren about God's work in your life in the past and help them see what He is doing right now to form the foundation for their belief and trust in God.*

Note 787. *Thanksgiving exalts God, gives Him credit for what is due, and takes our eyes off ourselves as we focus them on God.*

Note 788. *Thanksgiving is my response to the goodness and graciousness of God* (**Psalm 116: 12, 17a**).

Note 789. *Thanksgiving is thanking God for what He has done.*

Note 790. *The Bible says it—and that settles it!*

Note 791. *The Christian's life is the world's Bible* (**2 Corinthians 3:3**).

Note 792. *The first need of a local church is to teach believers to pray.*

Note 793. *The golden rule never tarnishes.*

Note 794. *"The greatest agency put into man's hand is prayer. And to define prayer one must use the language of war. Peace language is not equal to the situation. The earth is in a state of war and is being hotly beseiged. Thus one must use war talk to grasp the fact with which prayer is concerned. Prayer from God's side is communication between Himself and His allies in the enemy country. True prayer moves in a circle. It begins with the heart of God and* *sweeps down into the human heart on earth, so intersecting the circle of the earth, which is the battlefield of prayer, and then goes back again to its starting point, having accomplished its purpose on the downward swing."* **S. D. Gordon**

Note 795. *"The greatest work that any of us can do for one another, whether young or old, is to teach the soul to draw its water from the wells of God."* **F. B. Meyer**

Note 796. *The Holy Spirit is our Teacher who enlightens the eyes of our hearts* (**Ephesians 1:18**).

Note 797. *The main thing is to keep the main thing the main thing.*

Note 798. *The* MEANS *of forgiveness and cleansing is the blood of Jesus; the* METHOD *is the confession of sin, done by a Christian.*

Note 799. *The most important command in the Bible for a believer is to be filled with the Spirit* (**Ephesians 5:18**).

Note 800. *The realization (awareness) of sin(s) is where Christian maturity begins.*

Note 801. *The responsibility of every steward is to be responsible for that to which he has been entrusted by God.*

Note 802. *The Sovereign God has ordained prayer as the tool to get His work done.*

Note 803. *The unlimited potential of prayer is reflected in the promises of God.*

Note 804. *The Word of God is but a mirror to see yourself as God sees you under the guidance of the Holy Spirit.*

Note 805. *There is more power in the open hand than in the clinched fist.*

Note 806. *True repentance includes a change of mind, a hatred and turning away from sin, and a willingness to make things right.*

Note 807. *Unless we believe in an unlimited God, we do not really believe in God at all.*

Note 808. *Upon confession of sins is forgiveness and cleansing—but you must receive both in order to experience* *joy and peace.*

Note 809. *We are to put on the whole armor of God; God doesn't put it on for us.*

Note 810. *We are wise to find a church home, move into the middle of* **1 Corinthians 13** *and stay for the duration.*

Note 811. *We do not judge Scripture; Scripture judges us.*

Note 812. *We need never fear the darkness of this world, for Christ the Light is ever within us.*

Note 813. *We mutter and sputter, we fume and we spurt; We mumble and grumble, our feelings get hurt; We can't understand things, our vision grows dim; When all that we need is A MOMENT WITH HIM.*

Note 814. *What is in your hand? God often uses ordinary things for extraordinary purposes* (**Exodus 4:2-4**).

Note 815. *You have heard of many who did too little for God, but have you ever heard of anyone who did too much?*

Note 816. *When it's hardest to pray, pray the hardest.*

Note 817. *When there is full confession, there is full cleansing.*

Note 818. *When you received Christ, the Holy Spirit became resident; now, let Him be president by yielding and surrendering to His control* (**Ephesians 5:18**).

Note 819. *Whom God would greatly exalt, He often first humbles.*

Note 820. *There's nothing wrong in having nothing to say, unless you insist on saying it.*

Note 821. *With God's strength behind you, you can face the job ahead of you with confidence.*

Note 822. *Worship is what we give back to God for what He has done.*

Note 823. *You will never have a meaningful, sustained prayer life apart from living the Spirit-filled life.*

Note 824. *Your talk walks and your walk talks; but your walk talks more than your talk talks.*

Note 825. *You will never meet a person God does not love.*

Note 826. *You will feel rich if you will count all the things you have that money cannot buy.*

Note 827. *You'll find that putting God in the center of your life is exactly where He belongs.*

Note 828. *Success in spiritual work is dependent on prayer—the work which must come before all other work* (**John 14:12-14**).

Note 829. *"You can do more than pray after you've prayed, but you can never do more than pray until you have prayed."* **S. D. Gordon**

Note 830. *"Let us understand that the church's noblest work, the greatest task she could ever undertake, is to be the outlet of God's will. For the church to be the outlet of God's will is for her to pray."* **Watchman Nee**

Note 831. *Walk with the King today.* **Dr. Robert Cook**

Note 832. *If prayer is anything, prayer is everything.*

Note 833. *A bone of contention has no place in the Body of Christ.*

Note 834. *A boy is the only thing God can use to make a man.*

Note 835. *A cheerful countenance has a lot of face value.*

Note 836. *A Christian is never off duty.*

Note 837. *A Christian life becomes stale without a fresh exposure to God's Word each day.*

Note 838. *A Christian is a person who is forgiven, forgiving, and for giving.*

Note 838. *Admitting your mistakes is never a mistake.*

Note 840. *A small boy said to his parents: "I'm going to pray now. Do you need anything?"*

Note 841. *A sense of humor is the body's best shock absorber.*

Note 842. *A temper displayed in public is indecent exposure.*

Note 843. *Adversity should never get the Christian down, except on his knees.*

Note 844. *All other means of grace are ineffectual unless* *connected with prayer.*

Note 845. *A pair of good ears will drain dry a hundred tongues.*

Note 846. *A quitter never wins, and a winner never quits.*

Note 847. *A successful witness is one who shares Christ in the power of the Holy Spirit and leaves the results to God.*

Note 848. *An alcoholic is an alcoholic because he took his first drink.*

Note 849. *Tomorrow's challenges are already on God's agenda.*

Note 850. *Anything worth having in life is worth working for."* **Mom Henry**

Note 851. *Arguments seldom settle things, but prayer changes things.*

Note 852. *At the end of the road, you'll meet God.*

Note 853. *Be careful with your tongue. Simply don't say something if it is not good because the spoken word, no matter how much regretted, can never be recalled.*

Note 854. *Be careful little tongue what you say because there's a Father up above who is looking down in love.*

Note 855. *Be careful little eyes what you see because there's a Father up above who is looking down in love.*

Note 856. *Be careful little feet where you go because there's a Father up above who is looking down in love.*

Note 857. *Be careful little hands what you do because there's a Father up above who is looking down in love.*

Note 858. *Better be alone than in bad company.*

Note 859. *Careful! Too much of prayer is asking instead of thanking!*

Note 860. *Change your prayer sometimes. You can wake up in the morning and say, "God, what can I do for you today?"*

Note 861. *Christians are mirrors to reflect the glory of Christ, and a mirror does not call attention to itself unless there are flaws in it.*

Note 862. *Christians need to pray two prayers: "Lord,*

give me light" and "Give me grace to walk in the light."

Note 863. *A mistake is evidence that someone has tried to do something.*

Note 864. *Christ's last act before death was winning a soul; His last command was to win souls; His last prayer was forgiveness for a soul.*

Note 865. *Civilized man has learned how to fly, but has lost the art of walking with God.*

Note 866. *Common honesty should be more common.*

Note 867. *Consider your spiritual gift a gift from the Lord. Handle and use carefully.*

Note 868. *Count that day lost whose low descending sun views no worthy act done.*

Note 869. *Criticism, like dynamite, ought to be exploded only where it will do some good.*

Note 870. *Do nothing that you would not like to be doing when Jesus comes.*

Note 871. *Earth has no sorrow that Heaven cannot heal.*

Note 872. *Easy street is still mighty hard to find.*

Note 873. *Every day is a day of exciting discovery for the Christian who mines the Scriptures as one would dig for gold or other precious stones.*

Note 874. *"Father, we serve You gladly because we love You dearly."*

Note 875. *Fear not tomorrow; God is already there.*

Note 876. *Give God all He asks; receive all He promises.*

Note 877. *Go to no place where you would not like to be found when Jesus comes.*

Note 878. *God does not ever have to put one of His children's requests on back order since there is always plenty in the Storehouse to meet every need.*

Note 879. *God didn't save you to sit down on the stool of do nothing and be ornamental; He saved you to serve and work.*

Note 880. *God didn't save you only to go to Heaven; if He had, He could have taken you to Heaven the moment you were were saved. He has work on earth you need to do.*

Note 881. *God never sends His child away disappointed.*

Note 882. *God will not do for you what He has given you strength to do for yourself.*

Note 883. *God wants a whole heart, but will accept a broken one.*

Note 884. *Gossip is ear pollution.*

Note 885. *Gossip is like mud thrown against a clean wall; it may not stick, but it leaves an ugly mark.*

Note 886. *"Grant that we may never seek to bend the straight to the crooked; i.e., Thy will to ours, but that we and all doers, may bend the crooked to the straight, our will to Thine, that Thy will may be done."* **Augustine**

Note 887. *Grow angry slowly. There's plenty of time.*

Note 888. *Hats off to the past; coats off to the future.*

Note 889. *He who does not pray when the sun shines will not know how to pray when the clouds come.*

Note 890. *Heaven is headquarters for the believer where all the supplies are kept which we will ever need.*

Note 891. *Hot tempers lead to cool friends.*

Note 892. *How busy is not so important as why busy. The bee is praised; the mosquito is swatted—both are busy.*

Note 893. *How rare it is to find a person quiet enough to hear God speak.*

Note 894. *I one day asked, "Why doesn't somebody do something?" Then, I realized I was that somebody.*

Note 895. *If Christianity is worth having, it is worth sharing.*

Note 896. *"God's in His Heaven, all's right with the world."* **Robert Browning**

Note 897. *If we worry, we do not trust; if we trust, we do not worry.*

Note 898. *If you are a Christian, God needs you! If you are not a Christian, you need God!*

Note 899. *If you must kill time, be sure it's your own.*

Note 900. *If you work for God, form a committee; if you work with God, form a prayer group.*

Note 901. *Initiative is to success what a lighted match is to a candle.*

Note 902. *Initial salvation is the beginning, not the end, of our journey toward God.*

Note 903. *"It is almost impossible to get Christians to attend a meeting where God is the only attraction."* **A. W. Tozer**

Note 904. *It is better to say a good thing about a bad fellow, than to say a bad thing about a good fellow.*

Note 905. *It's nice to be important, but it's more important to be nice.*

Note 906. *Knowledge is power only when it is put to use.*

Note 907. A prayer: *"Lay any burden upon me, Lord, only sustain me. Send me anywhere, only go with me; sever any tie but that which binds me to Thy service and to Thy heart."*

Note 908. *Lives of great men all remind us we can make our lives sublime; reading God's Word daily helps us in our upward climb.*

Note 909. *Make much of Jesus and He will make much of you.*

Note 910. *Man's ears are not made to shut, but his mouth is.*

Note 911. *Many a blunt word has a sharp edge which cuts deeply.*

Note 912. *Many folks quit trying during trying times.*

Note 913. *Many prayers end up in the dead-letter box because they lack sufficient direction; be specific is the rule.*

Note 914. *When you keep in tune with Christ, you can sing in the dark.*

Note 915. *Meekness is power under control.*

Note 916. *Never let yesterday use up too much of today.*

Note 917. *No man has a right to do wrong.*

Note 918. *No man is ever so tall or straight as when he bends over to lift up little children.*

Note 919. *No one has been able to stand up indefinitely* *under the weight of carrying a grudge.*

Note 920. *No one is poor who can by prayer open the storehouse of Heaven.*

Note 921. *No person is qualified for Heaven who does not confess that by nature he is qualified for Hell.*

Note 922. *Nothing is discussed more and practiced less than prayer.*

Note 923. *Nothing lies outside the reach of prayer except that which is out of the will of God.*

Note 924. *Nothing makes us love our enemies as much as praying for them.*

Note 925. *Nothing ruins the truth like stretching it.*

Note 926. *One must be emptied of self in order to be filled with God.*

Note 927. *Only you can damage your character.*

Note 928. *Our efficiency without His sufficiency is only deficiency.*

Note 929. *People are as friendly as you are.*

Note 930. *People can't be judged by what others say about them, but they can be judged by what they say about others.*

Note 931. *People do not care how much you know until they know how much you care.*

Note 932. *People may doubt what you say, but they will always believe what you are.*

Note 933. *People who do not believe in prayer often make an exception when trouble comes in their lives.*

Note 934. *Peter knew he had let Jesus down when he should have held Him up—an acknowledgement which was the starting point of his renewal.*

Note 935. *Pray for a poor memory when people are unkind.*

Note 936. *Prayer and praise are like the wings of a bird— both must work together.*

Note 937. *Prayer does not need proof; it needs practice.*

Note 938. *Prayer is measured by its depth, not its length.*

Note 939. *Prayer is the child's helpless cry to the Father's attentive ear.*

Note 940. *Prayer is the mortar that holds our house together.*

Note 941. *Prayer is the pause that empowers.*

Note 942. *Prayer is the place where burdens change shoulders.*

Note 943. *Prayer is the one weapon the enemy cannot duplicate or counterfeit.*

Note 944. *Productive prayer requires earnestness, not eloquence.*

Note 945. *Raised voices lower esteem. Hot tempers cool friendships. Loose tongues stretch truth. Swelled heads shrink influence. Sharp words dull respect.*

Note 946. *Read nothing that you would not like to be reading when Jesus comes back to earth.*

Note 947. *Say nothing that you would not like to be saying when Jesus comes back to earth.*

Note 948. *Smiles never go up in price nor down in value.*

Note 949. *Some tears are liquid prayers.*

Note 950. *Sooner or later, we will all need some foreign aid—the kind we get from prayer.*

Note 951. *Strength in prayer is better than length in prayer.*

Note 952. *Success in witnessing is simply sharing Christ in the power of the Holy Spirit and leaving the results to God.*

Note 953. *Swallow your pride occasionally—it's nonfattening.*

Note 954. *Talk to God; He is easier to talk to than most people.*

Note 955. *Tarry at a promise until God meets you there.*

Note 956. *Ten years from now, what will you wish you had done now?*

Note 957. *"The best place to pray for potatoes is on the end of a hoe handle."* **Bud Robinson**

Note 958. *The Bible gives us precepts to obey, promises to claim, and principles to follow.*

Note 959. *The Bible is the only mirror into which man can look and see himself as God sees Him.*

Note 960. *"The Bible is, to many, God's unopened letter."* **Charles Spurgeon**

Note 961. *The Bread of Life never becomes stale.*

Note 962. *The Christian life should be characterized by a daily journey toward intimacy—knowing and loving God more and more, deeper and deeper.*

Note 963. *The Dead Sea is the dead sea because it takes in and doesn't give out; Christians must guard against the same.*

Note 964. *The devil is never very far away when you are too busy to pray.*

Note 965. *The easiest person to deceive is one's self.*

Note 966. *The easiest thing to find is fault.*

Note 967. *The entrance to trouble is wide; the exits are narrow without God's help.*

Note 968. *The essence of prayer is a sense of need. If you are going to strut like the proverbial peacock, you are not ready to enter into an effective prayer life.*

Note 969. *The Lord loves a cheerful giver; also a grateful receiver.*

Note 970. *The man who walks with God always gets to his destination.*

Note 971. *The most important things in life are not things.*

Note 972. *"The only generation that can reach this generation is our generation."* **Oswald J. Smith**

Note 973. *The person who drinks one drink of intoxicating beverages is one drink drunk.*

Note 974. *The person who knows everything has a lot to learn.*

Note 975. *The person who stands neutral usually stands for nothing.*

Note 976. *The same resource Jesus had to use against Satan is available to you and me—the eternal Word of God.*

Note 977. *The time is never right to do the wrong.*

Note 978. *The tragedy of our day is not unanswered prayer, but unoffered prayer.*

Note 979. *The worse thing about crossing a bridge before you get to it is that it leaves you on the wrong side of the river.*

Note 980. *There are books that inform and books that reform, but only the Bible can transform.*

Note 981. *There are two things that are hard on the heart—running up stairs and running down people.*

Note 982. *There is a mission field across the sea, but there is another one across the street.*

Note 983. *They will not seek, they must be sought; they will not come, they must be brought; they will not study, they must be taught.*

Note 984. *To err means you're trying.*

Note 985. *"To find God's will is the greatest discovery; to know God's will is the greatest knowledge; to do God's will is the greatest achievement."* **George Truitt**

Note 986. *To make progress in your Christian life, use two oars—a faith oar and a work oar. To use only one oar on one side of the boat will only result in your going in a circle.*

Note 987. *To walk with God, we must make it a practice to talk to God.*

Note 988. *Trouble will drive you to prayer and prayer will drive away the trouble.*

Note 989. *True Christianity is holiness put into action; it is faith gone to work!*

Note 990. *True faith is always ground in God's Word.*

Note 991. *We always find time to do what we really believe is important.*

Note 992. *We grow old, not by living, but by losing interest in living.*

Note 993. *We pray because it is a sin not to pray.*

Note 994. *When God writes opportunity on one side of open doors, he writes responsibility on the other side.*

Note 995. *When our finite understanding meets God's infinite wisdom, the only appropriate response is worship and silence.*

Note 996. *When we sit at the table with the Lord and taste His heavenly food, the devil's cooking doesn't taste right anymore.*

Note 997. *"Where there is a will, there is a way."* **Mom Henry**

Note 998. *Witnessing is one beggar telling another where to find food.*

Note 999. *Work for the night is coming when man works no more.*

Note 1000. *"Be sure you look to your secret prayer; keep that up, whatever you do; the soul cannot prosper in the neglect of it. Apostasy lurks outside the closet door."* **Philip Henry**

A Tribute

He was in many ways a typical Appalachian mountain man—quiet, gentle, reflective—the kind who could sit down at the end of a cornfield row to talk to a neighbor letting the plow and horse stand there for hours.

A very uncomplicated man. Simple things brought him pleasure—strawberry ice cream, lunch at Long John Silver's and a trip into the mountains, the place of his origins. Although he had his left leg amputated several years ago, he was simply not a complainer!

He was my Dad.

He is not a stranger to those who have been in a prayer seminar. The illustration of bringing my earthly father pleasure has many times reminded those present that we are to bring our Heavenly Father pleasure—and prayer is a primary way to do that.

Sometime during his sleep in the early morning hours on Friday, December 14, 1984, Dad was stricken with a massive stroke. He never regained consciousness. Through an one-hundred hour vigil, his children and grandchildren waited while his body closed down getting ready for his exodus. He was very strong.

At 2:50 p.m. (EST) on Tuesday, December 18, with his precious hands in my left hand and his brow in my right hand, Dad quietly moved out of his body without a struggle. It was a beautiful moment! Out of the body, he quickly moved through the first heavens where the birds fly through the second heavens where the stars and constellations are into the third heaven where Jesus is (**2 Corinthians 5:1,8**). Glorious reunion and homecoming!

Funeral services were conducted at 2 p.m. on Thursday, December 20, at Hill's Union Church in the Sandy Ridge community in Jefferson County. I preached sharing the Word from the Lord which the Holy Spirit gave to me. Mona, our daughter, sang a medley emphasizing grace and "Day by Day" reminded us that daily strength is always provided.

His body was laid to rest beside my Mom's body in that country cemetery which we so often visited together to await the return of the Lord Jesus Christ with His children. At that time, his body will stand up straight—the meaning of the word "resurrection"—move out of the grave first along with all other believers and go into the heavens. He will move back into his resurrected body, as will all other believers. Then Jesus will touch His children and each will have a body just like Christ's body. GLORIOUS! Any believers alive on earth will be caught up and will also have their bodies changed.

As long as there is a prayer seminar ministry, my Dad will continue to be a reminder that PRAYER BRINGS PLEASURE TO OUR HEAVENLY FATHER! It is our duty to do what brings both our earthly father and our Heavenly Father pleasure.

Reflector
Vol. XXXI, No. 1
January 1985

A Tribute

You can judge a person by what she loves!
Having been in the Troutman family three and one-half decades, my own memories are intensely active as I wander down reminiscent trail to recall thirty-six years of observation of a very remarkable woman, wife, mother, grandmother, and great-grandmother—my mother-in-law—Willie Clark King Troutman.

1. She loved God the Father, God the Son the Lord Jesus Christ, and the Holy Spirit as revealed in Creation, the Word of God, and her daily walk with them. Never was there a question about that which motivated her on a daily basis.

You can judge a person by what she loves!
Mrs. Troutman loved the Lord!

2. She loved the written Word—to hear, read, study, memorize, and meditate—and to talk about it. Whether it was the Scripture itself, sermons written in the *Sword of the Lord* or messages over the radio or diligent, formal study to prepare to teach her Sunday school class or informal study to feed her soul, she was never far from the Bible. She knew the Scriptures by heart and often there were opportunities for in-depth discussion of the meat of the Word in spiritual maturity far beyond what one would expect of a woman living in Troutman Hills, McLean County, Kentucky. She never settled for the milk of the Word, but wanted to understand the deep things of the Lord.

For her, great truths were settled because of the plain teaching of the Bible.

During the long months of winding down her earthly sojourn, Sue spent time reading Scriptures to her. Often, she needed only to begin a verse and her mother would finish it! Her long years of hiding the Word in her heart served her well.

Christian literature was important to her and her mailbox was full of publications which she read and frequently passed on to others. Often I have returned home from a visit with many wonderful articles to study.

You can judge a person by what she loves! Mrs. Rollie A. Troutman loved the Word!

3 . She loved her church. "Assembling together" at Old Buck Creek Baptist Church was important to her and she wanted to keep the doors open. Even when health began to fail, she wanted to be carried to the church. I can see her now dressed up in her church clothes with eyes that were sparkling and twinkling and a smile on her lips as she set out for church. She loved her pastor and had always an encouraging word. Singing, praying, giving, hearing the Word preached delighted her heart.

You can judge a person by what she loves! Willie Troutman loved the church of the Lord Jesus Christ.

4. She loved the causes of the Lord Jesus Christ. Her radio was tuned in to Ernest I. Reveal, Evansville Rescue Mission, and she talked of her interest in this ministry. All during the child-rearing years, the day started at 6:15 a.m. with Cadle Tabernacle's Nation's Family Prayer Period with a message by B. R. Lakin. "Ere you left your room this morning, Did you think to pray?" drifted through her home as the children prepared for the day. Back to the Bible and Theodore Epp were favorites. A few years ago when I conducted a prayer seminar for the staff of Back to the Bible, she was delighted. She was a staunch supporter of Dr. John R. Rice and the *Sword of the Lord*. Often she shared thoughts from the *Sword*—and sermons. The Old Time Gospel Hour became an item of interest when my family and I moved to Lynchburg, Virginia, to assist Dr. Jerry Falwell in establishing Liberty Baptist College. Her checkbook entries reflected her commitment.

Her partnership in the prayer seminar ministry in faithful giving and praying which has resulted in providing around 520 prayer seminars around the world has been remarkable. There has never been any doubt that she walked in her heart with Sue and me mile by mile.

You can judge a person by what she loves! Grandma Troutman loved the causes of the Lord Jesus Christ.

5. She loved her nation and her Kentucky. She expressed her concern for the moral decline of her country and felt that Kentucky was the best. She loved Troutman Hills and often joked that she was blessed by having several addresses starting with Livia and never having moved! She enjoyed her flowers and her garden!

You can judge a person by what she loves! Willie Clark King Troutman loved her land.

6. Then, she loved her family. Her husband of sixty-one years. Thirteen children. 27 grandchildren. 20 great-grandchildren. She had her family in her heart, in her mind, and in her prayers constantly. Their joys and victories were her joys and victories. Their sadnesses and defeats were her sadnesses and defeats. Her faith never wavered. Her interest reflected itself in constant letter-writing.

My fascination with her came during my first visit in 1956. She was prepared with a table ladened with delectable foods including a pineapple pudding. When we sat at the table, she expressed her appreciation to have a young preacher at her table, but she stated that she always served the most important one in her home first—her husband. Then the preacher would be served. Her devotion to "Pap" was unparalleled and touched my own heart more than words can tell.

Having her family gather for a Thanksgiving feast and for Christmas were highlights of her life for many years. As the grandchildren came, it was amazing that each grandchild was on her shopping list for Christmas—even when the number grew large. When others were asleep, she was still up working. She is the only person that I ever saw who gave herself so fully that she could fall asleep with a cup of coffee in her hand!

She enjoyed having her grandchildren visit her. It is said that children need to learn twenty percent of their life's values from grandparents. Mrs. Troutman was a teacher, whether it was teaching a daughter-in-law to make gravy without lumps or her granddaughter, Melody, how to cook using a "pinch" of this and a "dash" of that. Although Scrabble was her favorite game, she knew how to play a good game of "Husker Doo." She knew how to listen and encourage.

Soon time will pass and life will go on with routines and other crises. Let it be said, however, that the legacy of Mrs. Rollie A. Troutman (Willie Clark King) is one which will live on in the lives of many of us who have walked with her and were the recipients of her influence and good will. Our Lord said that when a believer does well that He will say "Well done, good and faithful servant." In my heart, there is assurance that Mrs. Troutman did well and will hear the accolade!

Genesis 2:7 and **1 Thessalonians 5:23.** A person is soul, spirit, and body. The body is the tabernacle that houses the person who is soul-spirit. Soul is mind, emotion, and will. The spirit is that part where the control seat is and where the Holy Spirit makes His residence when a person comes to Christ. The spirit of man died to God when Adam sinned (**Genesis 3**), but comes alive when a person is born again (**John 3**). The body and soul are not born again, but it is possible when we allow the Holy Spirit to control our lives for body and soul (mind, emotions, and will) to be controlled by the Holy Spirit. That is the goal of all of us.

The word "death" means separation when the person who lives inside the body (the real person) moves out. The Christian goes through the first heavens where the birds fly through the second heaven where the stars are and into the third heaven where Jesus is. Paul clearly tells us this in **2 Corinthians 5:1,8** when he says when this earthly house of this tabernacle is dissolved (that is, the earthly body), we have a body not made by hands eternal in the heavens (v 1). He climaxes this by revealing that to "be absent from the body is to be present with the Lord (v 8).

So what happened on Thanksgiving afternoon, November 26, was that Willie Troutman moved out of her earthly house (escorted by angels, by the way!), soared through the first and second heavens, and entered into the presence of the Lord in all its glory and splendor—in fact so great it is that "eye hath not seen, ear hath not heard, nor even entered into the minds of men the things He has laid up for His children" (**1 Corinthians 2:9**). At the same time, her death was "precious in the sight of the Lord" (**Psalm 116:15**).

The real person who moves into Heaven is fully conscious and is substantive. Therefore in Heaven, she will know and be known (**1 Corinthians 13:12**). I believe when Mrs. Troutman arrived home—not only our Lord Jesus Christ greeted her, but Genie, Ann, Grant Wade and other loved ones as well!

But that is not the end! One day the Lord Jesus Christ will return. When He does, He will bring into the air with Him those who have already gone to Heaven. Down on earth, the "dead will rise first" (1 **Thessalonians 3:13-18**) which means that those bodies which have been laid aside will now come to resurrection (the word "**resurrection**" means "**stand up straight**"). Those resurrection bodies will move into the air and the folks from Heaven will move back into their bodies. But that is not the rest of the story. It will be at that moment that the Lord will touch those resurrected bodies and make them glorified ones—bodies which will be just like Jesus' body (**1 John 3:2-3**). Thus shall we ever be with the Lord! Praise God!

Now as for those who are left behind, remember that Jesus promised that He would never leave us "comfortless" which is a Greek word—literally "orphans" (**John 14:18**). You and I are not orphans because the Holy Spirit is the "Comforter" Who came when Jesus returned to Heaven (**John 14:16**) to be the Paraclete (which is the Greek word translated "Comforter") and literally means One called along side to help—our Helper. Then in verse 17, Jesus explained to His disciples there in the Upper Room just hours before His death on the cross, that when the Holy Spirit came that He would be "in" us. What more can we ask! Expect the Holy Spirit to represent the Lord Jesus Christ well to meet your every need. Expect the Scriptures to come alive as never before as the Holy Spirit applies those Scriptures to your hearts. I know that He will.

Dr. J. Gordon Henry
Murfreesboro, Tennessee
November 28, 1992

Note: During Mom Troutman's funeral service, Rollie King Troutman, the eldest son, shared the following reading as a tribute to his mother on behalf of all the children.

A Mother's Love

A young mother set her feet on the pathway of life. *"Is the way long?"* she asked.

And her guide said, *"Yes, and the way is hard and you will be old before you reach the end of it, but the end will be better than the beginning."* But the young mother was happy and would not believe that anything could be better than these years. So she played with her children and gathered flowers for them along the way and bathed with them in the clear springs. The sun shone on them and life was good and the young mother cried, *"Nothing will be lovelier than this."*

Then the night came and the storms and the path was dark and the children shook with fear and cold. And the mother drew them close and covered them with her mantle, and the children said, *"Oh, mother, we are not afraid, for you are near and we know that no harm can come to us."* And the mother said, *"This is better than the brightness of the day, for I have taught my children courage."*

And the morning came and there was a hill ahead, and the children climbed and grew weary, and the mother was weary too, but at all times she said to the children, *"A little patience and we are there."* So the children climbed and climbed and when they reached the top, they said, *"Mother, we could not have done it without you."* And when the mother lay down to sleep that night, she looked up at the stars and said, *"This is a better day than the last, for my children have learned fortitude in the face of hardness. Yesterday, I gave them courage—today I gave them strength."*

And the next day the strange clouds came, clouds of war and hate and evil. And the children groped and stumbled, but the mother said, *"Look up. Lift up your eyes to the Light."* And the children looked up and saw above the clouds the Everlasting Glory and it guided them and brought them beyond the darkness. And that night the mother said, *"This is the best day of all, for I have shown my children God."*

And the days went on and the years and the mother grew old, and she was little and bent. But her children were tall and strong and walked with courage. And when the way was hard, they helped their mother and when the way was tough, they lifted her, for she was as light as a feather. And at last they came to a hill and beyond the hill they could see a shining road and gates flung wide and the mother said, *"I have reached the end of my journey and I know that the end is better than the beginning, for my children can walk alone, and their children after them."* And the children said, *"You will always walk with us, mother, even when you have gone through the gates."*

And they stood and watched her as she went on alone and the gates closed after her and they said, *"We cannot see her but she is with us still. A mother like ours is more than a Memory—she is a Living Presence."*

Favorite Poems

Over the years, I have used poems which have touched my heart and have become favorites.   Not only have I returned to them for my own encouragement, inspiration, and comfort, I have included them in my teaching-preaching ministry. Poems communicate.

Since 1955, God has allowed me to publish a paper called *The Reflector* which wends its way into thousands of homes across the nation. From the first issue, my intention has been to provide my readers with both information and inspiration. There is no better vehicle for inspiration than a poem which touches the heart.

Poems are made to share with others. My prayer is that you will be blessed by a few of my favorite poems and that you will pass them along to your family, friends, and even to the stranger who comes into your life.

The Bridge Builder

An old man, going a lone highway,
Came at the evening, cold and gray,
To a chasm, vast, and deep and wide,
Through which was flowing a sudden tide.
The old man crossed in the twilight dim
The sullen stream had no fears for him.
But he turned when safe on the other side,
And built a bridge to span the tide.

"Old man," said a fellow pilgrim near,
"You are wasting your strength building here.
Your journey will end with the closing day.
You will never again pass this way.
You have crossed this chasm deep and wide,
Why build you a bridge at even-tide?"

The builder lifted his old gray-head:
"Good friend, in the path I have come," he said,
"There followeth after me today,
A youth, whose feet must pass this way.
This chasm that has been naught to me,
To that fair-haired youth may a pitfall be,
He, too, must come in the twilight dim.
Good friend, I am building a bridge for him."

Selected

Key verse:
"I have shown you all things, how that so laboring ye ought
to support the weak, and to remember the words of the Lord
Jesus, how He said, *'It is more blessed to give than to
receive'* (**Acts 20:35**)."

70

The Camel

The camel at close of day
Kneels down upon the sandy plain
To have his burden lifted off
    And rest again.
MY SOUL
Thou too shouldest to thy knees,
When daylight draweth to a close,
And let the Master lift thy load.
    And grant repose.
ELSE HOW CANST THOU TOMORROW MEET
With all tomorrow's work to do,
If thou thy burden all the night
    Doest carry through?
The camel kneels at break of day
To have his guide replace the load;
Then rises up anew to take
    The desert road.
SO THOU
Shouldest kneel at morning's dawn,
That God may give thee daily care;
Assured that He no load too great
    Will make thee bear.

Selected

The Touch Of The Master's Hand

Twas battered and scarred, and the auctioneer
Thought it scarcely worth his while,
To waste much time on the old violin,
But held it up with a smile.
"What am I bid, good folks," he cried,
"Who'll start the bidding for me?"
"A dollar, a dollar;" then, *"Two! Only two?*
Two dollars, and who'll make it three?
Three dollars once; three dollars, twice;
Going for three—" But no,
From the room, far back, a gray-haired man
Came forward and picked up the bow;
Then, wiping the dust from the old violin,
And tightening the loose strings,
He played a melody pure and sweet
As a caroling angel sings.

The music ceased, and the auctioneer,
With a voice that was quiet and low,
Said, *"What am I bid for the old violin?"*
And he held it up with the bow.
"A thousand dollars, and who'll make it two?
Two thousand! And who'll make it three?
Three thousand, once; three thousand, twice,
And going, and gone," said he.
The people cheered, but some of them cried,
"We do not quite understand
What changed its worth," Swift came the reply;
"The touch of a master's hand."

And many a man with life out of tune,
And battered and scarred with sin,
Is auctioned cheap to the thoughtless crowd,
Much like the old violin.
A "mess of pottage," a glass of wine;
A game—and he travels on.
He is "going" once, and "going" twice,
He's "going" and almost "gone."
But the Master comes, and the foolish crowd
Never can quite understand
The worth of a soul and the change that's wrought
By the TOUCH OF THE MASTER'S HAND.

Myra Brooks Welch

A Builder or a Wrecker

I watched them tearing a building down,
A gang of men in a busy town.
With a ho-heave-ho and a lusty yell,
They swung a beam and a side wall fell.
I asked the foreman, *"Are these men skilled?*
And the men you'd hire if you had to build?"
He gave a laugh and said, *"No indeed!*
Just common labor is all I need.
I can easily wreck in a day or two
What builders have taken a year to do."
And I thought to myself as I went my way,
Which of these roles have I tried to play?
Am I a **builder** who works with care,
Measuring life by the rule and square?
Am I shaping my deeds to a well-made plan,
Patiently doing the best I can?
Or am I a **wrecker**, who walks the town,
Content with the labor of tearing down?

Selected

74

Overheard in an Orchard

Said the Robin to the Sparrow:
"I should really like to know
Why these anxious human beings
Rush around and worry so?"

Said the Sparrow to the Robin:
"Friend, I think that it must be
That they have no Heavenly Father
Such as cares for you and me."

"Behold the fowls of the air; for they sow not, neither do
they reap, nor gather into barns; yet your Heavenly Father
feedeth them. Are ye not much better than they?"
Matthew 6:26

The Difference

I got up early one morning
And rushed right into the day;
I had so much to accomplish
That I didn't have time to pray.
Problems just tumbled about me,
And heavier came each task.
"Why doesn't God help me?," I wondered,
He answered, *"You didn't ask."*
I wanted to see joy and beauty,
But the day toiled on, gray and bleak,
I wondered why God didn't show me.
He said, *"But you didn't seek."*
I tried to come into God's presence;
I used all my keys at the lock.
God gently and lovingly chided,
"My child, you didn't knock."
I woke up early this morning,
And paused before entering my day,
I had so much to accomplish
That I had to take time to pray.

Author unknown

He Maketh No Mistake

My Father's way may twist and turn,
My heart may throb and ache,
But in my soul I'm glad I know,
He maketh no mistake.

My cherished plans may go astray,
My hopes may fade away,
But still I'll trust the Lord to lead,
For He doeth know the way.

Tho night be dark and it may seem,
That day will never break,
I'll pin my faith, my all in Him,
He maketh no mistake.

There's so much now I cannot see,
My eyesight far too dim,
But come what may, I'll simply trust
And leave it all to Him.

For by and by the mist will lift,
And plain it all He'll make,
Through all the way, tho dark to me,
He made not one mistake.

Author Unknown

Sermons We See

I'd rather see a sermon than hear one
    any day,
I'd rather one should walk with me
    than merely show the way.
The eye's a better pupil and more willing
    than the ear;
Fine counsel is confusing, but example's
    always clear;
And the best of all the preachers are
    the men who live their creeds,
For to see the good in action is what
    everybody needs.
I can soon learn how to do it if you'll
    let me see it done.
I can watch your hands in action, but
    your tongue too fast may run.
And the lectures you deliver may be
    very wise and true;
But I'd rather get my lesson by observing
    what you do.
For I may misunderstand you and the
    high advice you give,
But there's no misunderstanding how
    you act and how you live.

Edgar A. Guest

Wholly Thine

Write Thy name on my HEAD,
    That I may THINK for Thee;
Write Thy name on my LIPS,
    That I may SPEAK for Thee.

Write Thy name on my FEET,
    That I may WALK for Thee;
Write Thy name on my HANDS,
    That I may WORK for Thee.

Write Thy name on my EARS,
    That I may LISTEN for Thee;
Write Thy name on my HEART,
    That I may LOVE for Thee.

Write Thy name on my EYES,
    That I may SEE for Thee;
Write Thy name on my SHOULDERS,
    That I may BEAR BURDENS for Thee.

WRITE THY NAME ALL OVER ME,
    THAT I MAY BE WHOLLY THINE.

                    Dr. B. H. Carroll

Step by Step

He does not lead me year by year,
    Nor even day by day;
But step by step my path unfolds,
    My Lord directs my way.

Tomorrow's plans I do not know,
    I only know this minute;
But He will say, *"This is the way,*
By faith now walk ye in it."

And I am glad that it is so;
    Today's enough to bear;
And when tomorrow comes, His grace
    Shall far exceed its cares.

What need to worry then or fret;
    The God Who gave His Son,
Holds all my moments in His hand,
    And gives them one by one.

Selected

I Am His and He is Mine

Heaven above is softer blue,
Earth around is sweeter green;
Something lives in every hue,
Christless eyes have never seen!
Birds with gladder songs overflow,
Flowers with deeper beauties shine,
Since I know, as now I know,
I am His and He is mine.

Wade Robinson

Could I Be Called a Christian?

Could I be called a Christian,
If everybody knew,
My secret thoughts and feelings
In everything I do?
Or could they see the likeness
Of Christ in me each day?
Or could they hear Him speaking,
In every word I say?

Could I be called a Christian
If everyone could know
That I am found in places
Where Jesus would not go?
Or could they hear His echo
In every song I sing?
In eating, drinking, dressing,
Could they see Christ in me?

Could I be called a Christian
If judged by what I read?
By all my recreations,
And every thought and deed?
Could I be counted Christlike
As I now work and pray?
Unselfish, kind, forgiving
To others every day?

NOTE: I first used this poem in the **Liberty Avenue Baptist Reflector** in 1955. Some of you who have been receiving **The Reflector** over the years will recognize it. It is just as appropriate four decades later as it was then.

Be Careful What You Say

In speaking of another's faults,
    Pray don't forget your own.
Remember those with houses of glass
    Should never throw a stone;
If we have nothing else to do
    But talk of those who sin,
Tis better we commence at home,
    And from that spot begin.

We have no right to judge a man,
    Until he's fairly tried;
Should we not like his company,
    We know the world is wide.
Some may have faults and who has not?
    The old as well as the young,
Perhaps we may, for aught we know,
    Have fifty to their one.

I'll tell you of a better plan,
    And find it works far well,
To try my own defects to cure,
    Before of others tell;
And though I sometimes hope to be
    No worse than those I know
My own shortcomings bid me
    Let the faults of others go.

Then let us all, when we commence
    To slander friends or foe
Think of the harm one word may do
    To those we little know.
Remember, curses, like our chickens,
    Sometimes "roost at home."
Don't speak of others' faults
    Until we have none of our own.

On Your Anniversary

Note: The following poem was written by Mrs. Lloyd Kirby (Celia) upon the second anniversary of Dr. Henry as pastor of the Kerby Knob Baptist Church (KY) in October 1964 and appeared in **The Kerby Knob Baptist Reflector** on November 20, 1966. JGH

I do not have a card for your anniversary,
    Nor can I write a poem;
But what you have meant to me these past two years,
    Only God and I have known.

We have seen many things accomplished
    As these two years flew by;
We have heard the children singing
    And have seen the old ones cry.

We have seen our church so humble
    Grown into a house so fine
Where we can sit in comfort
    And sing the songs of Zion.

It has been my pleasure to know you
    And my heart often fills with joy
Just to hear you preach the Gospel
    To our lost girls and boys.

When we were like the lost in Egypt
    With our hearts asleep and cold,
God sent us a Moses to awake
    And unlock our hearts' door.

It has meant so much to me
    As you preached with a smile
So that the love of Jesus penetrated
    The heart of every little child.

And to see souls give their hearts
    To Jesus at the very water's edge
And say they wanted to be buried

Just like their Lord had said.

How you have prayed beside the sick bed
　　As you held a fevered hand;
And it make us rejoice greatly
　　That God has given to us such a man.

And to know your love for others
　　As you went far and near
Just to comfort a broken heart
　　Who had lost someone so dear.

May God's richest blessings be
　　On you and yours,
And our hearts and church forever
　　Be to you an open door.

Do It Now

If you have a piece of labor,
    Do it now;
If you want to show a favor,
    Show it now.

Do not put it off a day,
Chances do not always stay,
Do your duty while you may,
    Do it now.

If you would some pathway brighten,
    Do it now;
Or a heavy load to lighten,
    Do it now.

There is trouble everywhere,
Hearts are laden down with care,
If you would their burdens share,
    Do it now!

                              Selected

The New Leaf

He came to my desk with quivering lip,
    The lesson was done.
"Have you a new leaf for me, dear teacher,
    I have spoiled this one."
I took his leaf, all soiled and blotted
    And gave him a new one, all unspotted,
Then into his tired heart I smiled,
    "Do better now, my child."

I went to the throne with trembling heart,
    The year was gone.
"Have you a new year for me, dear Master,
    I have spoiled this one."
He took my year, all soiled and blotted
    And gave me a new one, all unspotted,
Then, into my tired heart He smiled,
    "Do better now, my child."

Selected

Better than a Light

I said to the man
     At the gate of the New Year,
"Give me a light that I
     May tread safely into the unknown."
And he replied:
     "Go out into the darkness and
PUT YOUR HAND INTO THE HAND OF GOD.
That shall be to you BETTER THAN A LIGHT,
And safer than the known way.

                              Selected

A Word

A word is dead
When it is said,
   Some say.
I say it just
Begins to live
   That day.

Emily Dickinson

Three Gates

If you are tempted to reveal
A tale to you someone has told
About another, make it pass,
Before you speak, three gates of gold.

These narrow gates: First, *IS IT TRUE?*
Then, *IS IT NEEDFUL?* In your mind
Give truthful answer. And the next
Is last and narrowest, *IS IT KIND?*

And if to reach your lips at last
It passes through these gateways three,
Then you may take the tale, nor fear
What the result of speech may be.

From *Arabian*

Try Prayer

The snow-coated crown of the mountain crest
Rose majestically into the sky;
It seemed it could stand there forever,
With time passing endlessly by.
And I thought there was nothing more stable,
Stubbornly resisting erosion and wear.
Then a still, small voice spoke to my heart:
"Have you ever relied upon prayer?"

The warmth and glow of an autumn day
Filled the earth with a beauty rare;
As the caw of a crow on a cornfield raid
Joining the honking of geese in the air.
Now my senses were soothed in an uncommon way;
I had found comfort, sweet and most rare.
Then the voice again whispered in my ear:
"You'll find more comfort in prayer."

The ocean roared like an untamed beast,
With a fury that could not be restrained.
And I shuddered at the vast power it possessed,
Whose source could not be explained.
As I watched the waves breaking high and wild,
To confront it I never would dare.
Once more I heard that mysterious voice:
"Have you experienced the power of prayer?"

The lake was tranquil at the close of day;
Not a ripple disturbed its bright face,
Dyed a fiery red by a fast-setting sun,
While a frog was tuning his nocturnal bass,
And all life seemed to be holding its breath.
Surely no greater peace could exist anywhere.
But the voice corrected my thoughts:
"You'll find greater peace in prayer."

Sunrise! How glorious was the dawn,
O'er all the earth and by the shining sea;

Waking the little folds of field and forest;
Calling to his daily labor man and bee.
It spoke of promise for the future,
And also hope, to me by far most fair.
"My friend," the voice spoke so gently to me:
"You'll find the source of hope is really prayer."

Having experience all these earthly glories,
One thing more I craved—to draw apart
And have communion with my Heavenly Father;
To meet Him in the temple of my heart
And worship Him with purest adoration.
With this no other thing could e'er compare.
The voice now sounded sweet and holy:
"You can meet Him any time in sincere prayer."

Willis James Snow
Waterford, Connecticut

Note: Willis shared this poem with us when he was eighty-eight years old, a few months before his death on September 16, 1991 just prior to his ninetieth birthday. For many years, Willis ministered to me through correspondence. He was an encourager in each letter and always included at least one page of humor. What an amazing intellect! What a tremendous facility to put thoughts into words. In all my work in higher education with many excellent students sitting in my classes, none was in Willis' category. He was a literary genius. He and his wife, Carol, became **Doorkeepers** in August 1983.

In a letter dated March 28, 1987, Willis shared: *"Just as a matter of curiosity, I took a census. I enumerated the people for whom I pray every day and it totaled 217. In addition to these, there are invariably five to a dozen each day which are acute cases and need immediate intercession. This would include people undergoing surgery, a bereavement, an accident, or things of this nature which are usually not on-going situations. I bring each one individually to the throne of grace and do not present them in platoons. Does all praying require time? It sure does, but time can never be spent more profitably."* The prayer seminar ministry was on that list.

To say I have missed Willis Snow would be an understatement. Knowing he is as interested in our work in Heaven as he was on earth certainly motivates me to give my best.

I'll Go—Maybe!

I'll go where You want me to go, dear Lord.
    Real service is what I desire.
I'll sing a solo any time, dear Lord,
    But please don't ask me to sing in the choir.

I'll do what You want me to do, dear Lord.
    I like to see things come to pass.
But don't ask me to teach girls and boys, dear Lord,
    I'd just rather stay in my class.

I'll do what You want me to do, dear Lord.
    I long for Thy kingdom to thrive.
I'll give you nickels and dimes, dear Lord,
    But please don't ask me to tithe.

I'll go where you want me to go, dear Lord.
    I'll say what You want me to say.
I'm busy just now with myself, dear Lord,
    I'll help you some other day.

                        Selected

The Throne Room of Prayer

I'm no artist with canvas and brushes and oils—
Able to paint for the eye,
But in bright mental vision, with phrases and words
I paint and mind pictures supply.

This vision my heart wants to bring to your heart
With thoughts that my mind sends your way,
So in the imagining core of yourself
You can see, truly see, what I say.

I will draw you today to a place of great worth—
A wonderful spot I must share,
Where we enter as often and long as we like,
The heavenly Throne Room of Prayer!

The way there is easy, yet hard, both at once,
How can I desire something so,
Yet put it aside at any excuse
When its value I surely should know.

Transportation's arranged by our heavenly King
And of distance we're never aware.
From our knees or our feet or from our own beds
Just look up to God and we're there!

As we enter this room, holy awe fills our hearts
And we view only God and His ways.
In His presence, our pains and our cares are cast off
And His glorious beauty we praise.

As we focus the eyes of our spirits on Him
And the darkness and dullness and gloom
Of the earth fades behind us and we enter in—
And we realize—it's His Throne Room.

So great and majestic, our glorious Lord!
How can we dare to come near?
But He holds out His hand and says,

"My dear child, come closer, you need have no fear.

In My Son you have access, He brought you for Me.
There's nothing more you need to do,
So come and have fellowship. It's My desire.
I really do love and want you.

The song in your heart was put there by Me,
Its melody pleases Me so.
Rejoice in My goodness, My wonderful ways,
Then we'll talk more, our closeness will grow."

"But Lord, I am sinful. My heart is ashamed.
I see nothing but evil in me."
"Repent and confess, I'll forgive all the sin—
My forgiveness is boundless and free."

"I thank You, my God, for all you have done
Your goodness, compassion and care.
You meet all my needs and make all things good
Together we'll fellowship share.

My eyes have been looking at You, only You,
In all Your unchangeable grace.
But for some reason I'm now drawn to see
Something else besides Your lovely face."

A sorrowful figure, depressed and alone
Is standing just outside the door,
As I reach out a hand to draw that one in
I see there are so many more.

"Some are my family, some from my church,
Some know and love you, yet cry
'How can I handle the pressures of life?
The road is too hard, dear Lord. Why?'

Some have discouragements, problems, and doubts.
Some are by others abused.
Some simply don't know where to turn next,

Their minds are disturbed and confused.

Many are joyously serving You, Lord,
In lands far away or right here,
Telling the ones who don't know You at all,
But they also hurt, tire, and fear.

One is in terrible pain, near to death,
One is just seeking Your will.
One has temptations he battles alone
Climbing this long, hopeless hill.

These are the ones You have caused me to see.
For a reason, to hold them, in prayer
Up before You, my wonderful Lord,
For all of them You really care.

Oh, Lord, as I learn to come freely and oft
Into this wonderful place,
Help me remember to pray for the ones
You love and have saved by Your grace.

Help me remember not my needs alone
Though about them You surely do care,
But to hold up the needs of others as well
As I stand in the Throne Room of Prayer."

Marie Herling
El Cajon, CA

Marie has been a **Doorkeeper** partner in the prayer seminar ministry for many years. God has used her mightily in short-term ministry in Ukraine after her retirement as a nurse.

A Precious Discovery

In leafing through a book that belonged to my mother-in-law, Mrs. Rollie A. Troutman, who went home to be with the Lord on Thanksgiving Day, 1992, I found a page from a February 1955 desk calendar tucked away. May its message bring you the peace and comfort which it has brought me. You may want to tuck it away in one of your books—to enable a member of your family to experience a precious discovery to share with others after you, too, have gone to Heaven.

Thou, O Lord, knowest me

MY NAME
And He called His own sheep by name, and leadeth them.

John 10:3

MY THOUGHTS
Thou knowest my down sitting and mine uprising, Thou understandest my thought afar off.

Psalm 139:2

MY WAYS
But He knoweth the way that I take: when He hath tried me, I shall come forth as gold.

Job 23:10

MY PATH
The path of the just is as the shining light, that shineth more and more unto the perfect day.

Proverbs 4:18

MY NEEDS
Your Father knoweth what things ye have need of, before ye ask Him.

Matthew 6:8

Faith

Faith bids me trust
And not worry,
Faith bids me wait
And not hurry.
Faith bids me work
Without complaint.
Faith bids me share
His love untold.
Faith bids me hope
And not relent.
Faith bids me serve
'Till life is spent.

Mrs. Harmon Eggleston

What is faith? It is simply believing God will do what He says He will do. How much faith does one need to pray? Just enough that cause you to turn to God!

Faith does not save a person. What it does is to get a person to the Lord Jesus Christ, the Savior. Study **Ephesians 2:8-9** and **Hebrews 11:6**.

If the object of faith is any less than Jesus, one day the faith will fizzle.

The opposite of walking by faith is walking by sight. After we have exercised faith for salvation, we are to forever walk by faith until God calls us home to Heaven.

The Gospel According to You

You are writing a Gospel,
A chapter each day,
By deeds that you do,
By words that you say.

Men read what you write
Whether faultless or true;
Say, what is the gospel
According to you?

Selected

Prayer seminar helps you get started!

Most Christians know the important place of prayer in the life of a believer. I do not have to make a case with you about that.

But it is not easy to pray. It is easier to preach, to do youth work or the work of a deacon, to teach a Sunday school class, or to go visiting! Why is this?

I believe the reason Satan doesn't want a person to learn to pray is because prayer unleashes the power of God in the life of a believer. Satan trembles when he sees the weakest Christian on his knees. I will never win the war if I don't know where the battle is being fought. Prayer is the place!

What about your personal altar? Is it broken down and deserted? Take an inventory of your prayer life. What is happening in your life in answer to prayer? What about others in your church?

A prayer seminar could help you and other believers get started! Using the *Prayer Seminar Workbook* (79 pages), the six-hour prayer seminar teaches the importance of a proper and effective prayer life for the Christian and clearly demonstrates the spiritual impact every believer can generate through prayer. Over 900 seminars have been conducted in forty-five states, the District of Columbia, and forty nations:, Argentina, Australia, the Bahamas, Botswana, Brazil, Chile, China, Cuba, Costa Rica, England, Germany, Fiji Islands, India, Indonesia, Israel, Italy, Jamaica, Japan, Korea, Lesotho, Malaysia, Mexico, Mozambique, New Zealand, Nigeria, N. Ireland, Okinawa, the Philippines, Puerto Rico, Romania, Russia, Scotland, Singapore, South Africa, Swaziland, Switzerland, Thailand, Ukraine, Venezuela,, and Zambia.

HOW TO:
- Establish prayer as a daily priority.
- Organize your praying following a biblical pattern.
- Worship, praise, confess, and thank the Lord.
- Pray for yourself, as well as others.

The prayer seminar is a faith ministry that trusts God to provide the financial needs through local churches and individuals. Therefore, we do not charge a set fee. Basically, participants are encouraged to contribute a one-time gift through the church love offering for the seminar as the Lord leads. Each participant receives a copy of the prayer seminar workbook, the basic teaching tool. A suggested contribution is $5 to defray the printing cost. Beyond the free-will offering, help with travel is necessary. If the Lord lays on your heart to host a seminar, however, do not hesitate to make contact with J. Gordon Henry Ministries about the travel expense, if that is a problem.

Seminars have been conducted with Baptist (various groups), Christian and Missionary Alliance, Church of the Brethren, Free Brethren, Grace Brethren, Free Methodist, United Methodist, Presbyterian, Mennonite, Apostolic, Assembly of God, Church of God, Conservative Congregational, Christian, Pentecostal, Evangelical Free, Lutheran, Pentecostal Free Will Baptists, Reformed, Christian Reformed, Quakers (Friends), Salvation Army, and independent Bible churches. In addition, there have been seminars in Bible colleges and liberal arts/colleges/universities. Prayer seminars have been conducted for statewide men's retreats, summer camp meetings and/or retreats for special groups, such as pastors. Seminars have been conducted on military bases and in prisons.

For additional information about the seminar (including a sample copy of the workbook, letters of reference, and scheduling), write or call:

J. Gordon Henry Ministries

4:00 P.M.

1127 Lakeview Drive

Lynchburg, VA 24502-2807

(434) 239-8837 .org

email: jghm84@aol.com